Circulation and Exchange Patterns in Sinclair Inlet, Washington

By Marlene A. Noble, Kurt J. Rosenberger, Anthony J. Paulson, and Anne L. Gartner

Open-File Report 2013–1117

U.S. Department of the Interior
U.S. Geological Survey

U.S. Department of the Interior
SALLY JEWELL, Secretary

U.S. Geological Survey
Suzette M. Kimball, Acting Director

U.S. Geological Survey, Reston, Virginia: 2013

For more information on the USGS—the Federal source for science about the Earth,
its natural and living resources, natural hazards, and the environment—visit
http://www.usgs.gov or call 1–888–ASK–USGS

For an overview of USGS information products, including maps, imagery, and publications,
visit *http://www.usgs.gov/pubprod*

Suggested citation:
Noble, M.A., Rosenberger, K.J., Paulson, A.J., and Gartner, A.L., 2013, Circulation exchange patterns in Sinclair
Inlet, Washington: U.S. Geological Survey Open-File Report 2013-1117, 40 p.

Contents

Figures

Tables

Conversion Factors and Datums

Conversion Factors

SI to Inch/Pound

Multiply	By	To obtain
Length		
millimeter (mm)	0.03937	inch (in.)
centimeter (cm)	0.3937	inch (in.)
meter (m)	3.281	foot (ft)
meter (m)	1.094	yard (yd)
kilometer (km)	0.6214	mile (mi)
kilometer (km)	0.5400	mile, nautical (nmi)
Area		
square centimeter (cm^2)	0.001076	square foot (ft^2)
square kilometer (km^2)	247.1	acre
square kilometer (km^2)	0.3861	square mile (mi^2)
Volume		
cubic meter (m^3)	6.290	barrel (petroleum, 1 barrel = 42 gal)
Flow rate		
centimeter per second (cm/s)	0.3937	inch per second (in./s)
cubic meter per second (m^3/s)	70.07	acre-foot per day (acre-ft/d)
Mass		
gram (g)	0.03527	ounce, avoirdupois (oz)
kilogram (kg)	2.205	pound avoirdupois (lb)
Pressure		
bar	100	kilopascal (kPa)

Temperature in degrees Celsius (°C) may be converted to degrees Fahrenheit (°F) as follows: °F=(1.8×°C)+32.

Datum

Vertical coordinate information is referenced to the World Geodetic System of 1984 (WGS84) datum.

Circulation and Exchange Patterns in Sinclair Inlet, Washington

By Marlene A. Noble, Kurt J. Rosenberger, Anthony J. Paulson, and Anne L. Gartner

Introduction

In 1994, the U.S. Geological Survey (USGS), in cooperation with the U.S. Navy, deployed three sets of moorings in Sinclair Inlet, which is a relatively small embayment on the western side of Puget Sound (fig. 1). This inlet is home to the Puget Sound Naval Shipyard. One purpose of the measurement program was to determine the transport pathways and fate of contaminants known to be present in Sinclair Inlet. Extensive descriptions of the program and the resultant information about contaminant pathways have been reported in Gartner and others (1998). This report primarily focused on the bottom boundary layer and the potential for resuspension and transport of sediments on the seabed in Sinclair Inlet as a result of tides and waves.

Recently (2013), interest in transport pathways for suspended and dissolved materials in Sinclair Inlet has been rekindled. In particular, the USGS scientists in Washington and California have been asked to reexamine the datasets collected in the earlier study to refine not only our understanding of transport pathways through the inlet, but to determine how those transport pathways are affected by subtidal currents, local wind stress, and fresh water inputs. Because the prior study focused on the bottom boundary layer and not the water column, a reanalysis of the datasets could increase our understanding of the dynamic forces that drive transport within and through the inlet. However, the early datasets are limited in scope and a comprehensive understanding of these transport processes may require more extensive datasets or the development of a detailed numerical model of transport processes for the inlet, or both.

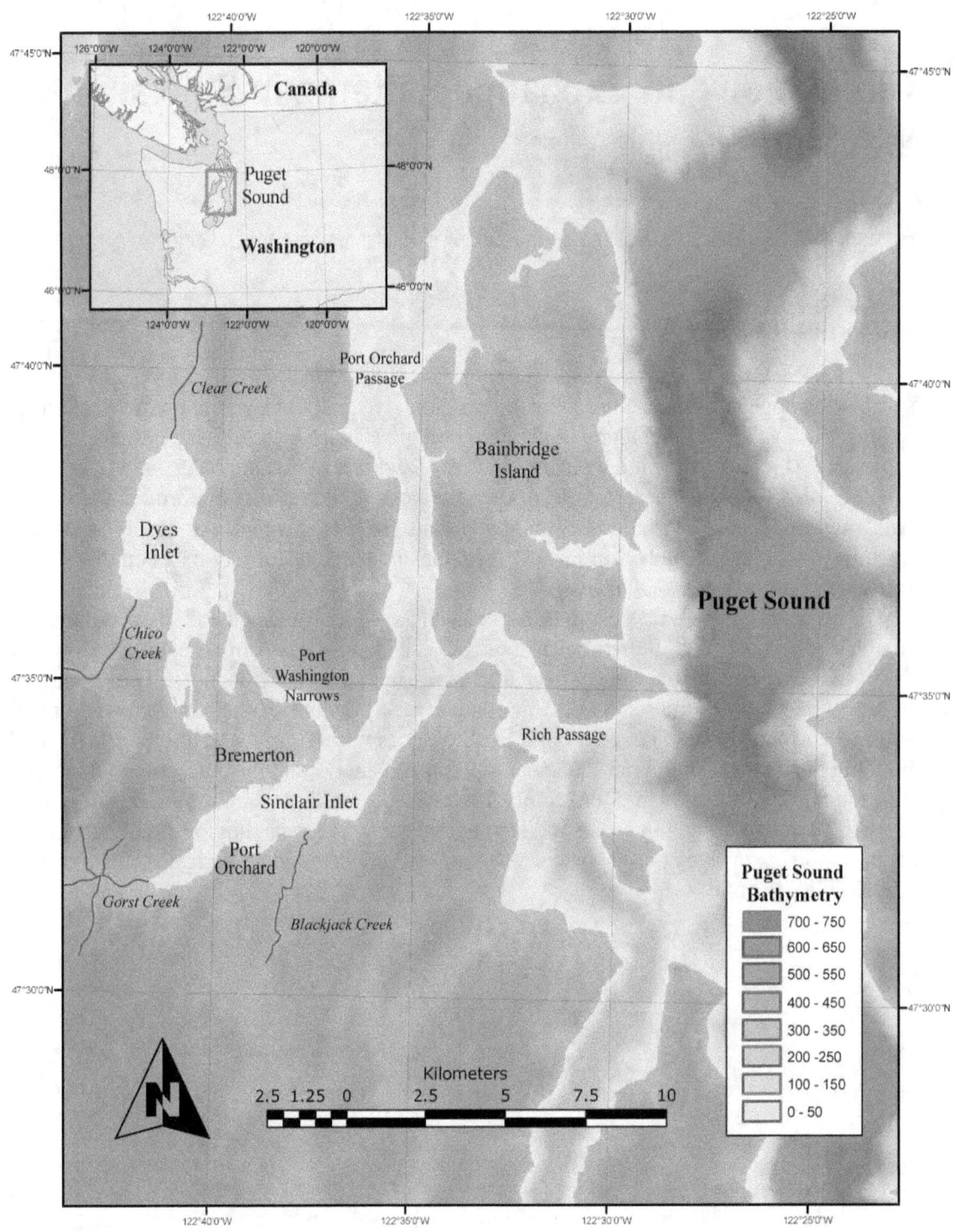

Figure 1. Map showing general location of Sinclair Inlet and relative position to the mouth of Puget Sound, Washington. Bathymetry contours are water depth below mean lower low water, in meters.

Regional Setting and Forcing

Sinclair Inlet is a relatively small inlet near Bremerton, Washington. The Puget Sound Naval Shipyard occupies about half of the northwestern shore of this inlet (fig. 2). The inlet is about 7 km long and 2 km wide. It is relatively shallow; depths in the center of the inlet generally are between 10 and 20 m. The major axis of the inlet is aligned about 65 degrees clockwise of north.

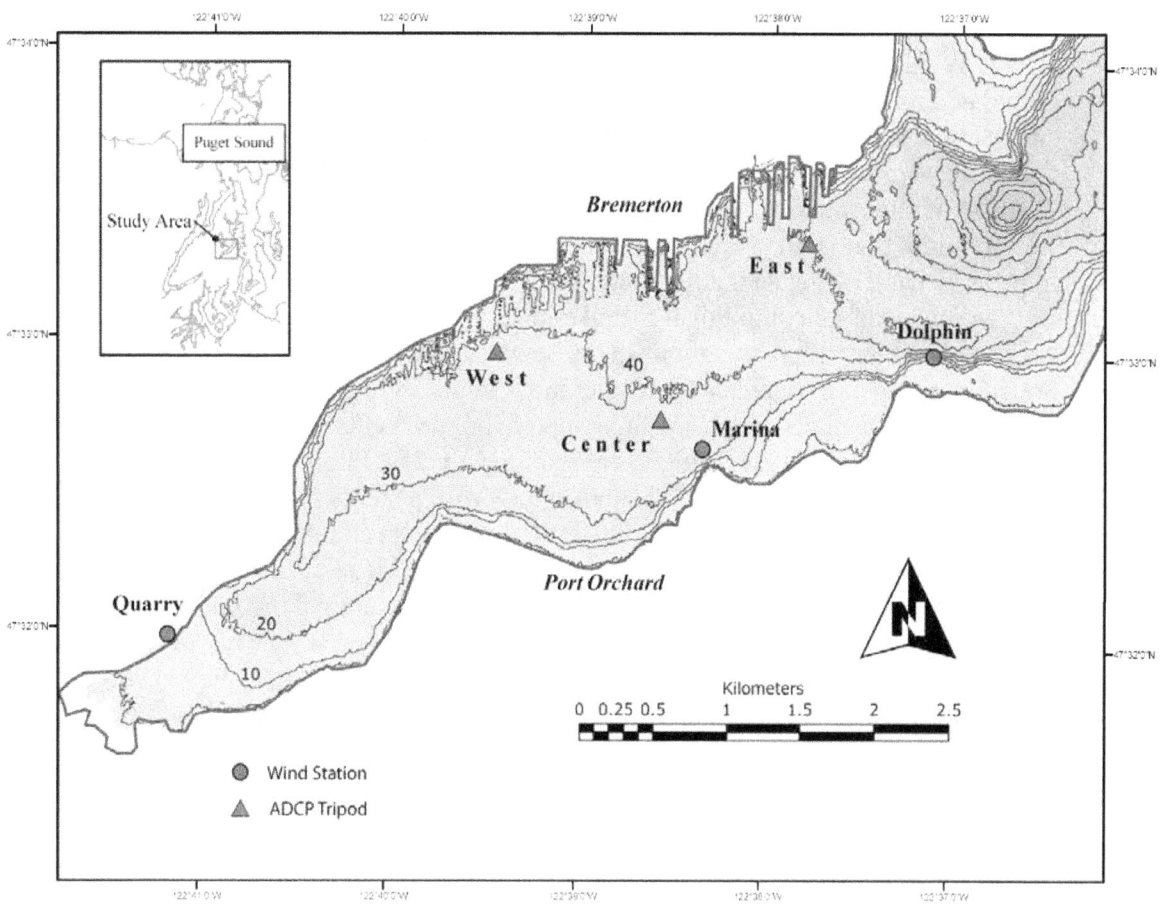

Figure 2. Map showing locations of the East, Center, and West acoustic Doppler current profilers (ADCP) tripod sites and wind measurement stations in Sinclair Inlet, Washington. Bathymetry contours are shown as water depth below mean lower low water, in feet.

Sinclair Inlet connects to Puget Sound via two passages: Rich Passage to the south of Bainbridge Island and Port Orchard Passage that extends along the western side of Bainbridge Island and connects to Puget Sound north of the island (fig.1). Thus, exchange and flushing of the estuary potentially has two pathways, although most exchange with Puget Sound is likely to occur through Rich Passage, which is closer and deeper than Port Orchard Passage. Another small inlet, Dyes Inlet, approximately the same size as Sinclair Inlet, connects to Sinclair Inlet via Port Washington Narrows along the northern shore, to the east of the Port of Bremerton. Therefore, any attempt to determine residence times

3

for the inlet must include the bodies of water connected to and between Sinclair Inlet and Puget Sound because there is no simple, direct connection to Puget Sound.

Winds in Puget Sound tend to be regional in scale, but exhibit local steering in individual inlets and passages. Wind direction tends to be northerly (that is, blowing towards the north) in the winter and southerly in the summer in Puget Sound (Overland and Walter, 1983). For Sinclair Inlet, this translates to a predominantly down-inlet (toward the mouth) winds in the winter and up-inlet winds in the summer. In addition, more significant diurnal heating and cooling in the summer leads to a high diurnal signal (or sea-breeze) during the summer months.

Winds and atmospheric pressure disturbances also can lead to water level anomalies in Puget Sound and its inlets. Finlayson (2005) demonstrated that Puget Sound responds to these anomalies as a single body, and surges are greater during the winter months (99 percent are between -40 and +60 cm) than in the summer months (99 percent are between -30 and +30 cm). Finlayson (2005) calculated from 20 years of atmospheric pressure and water-level data that the inverse barometer effect for Seattle is -19.4 mm/mb; that is, for a 1 mb rise in atmospheric pressure, the water level is likely to decline 19.4 mm. These water level anomalies could have implications for circulation and flushing in Sinclair Inlet.

Freshwater input to Puget Sound and its inlets is highly seasonal; rainfall generally occurs in the winter (85 percent of precipitation occurs between October and April). Although other regions of Puget Sound may experience higher freshwater input in the spring and summer because of snowmelt runoff, Sinclair Inlet is isolated from any direct input from rivers that deliver snowmelt. The watershed that drains into Sinclair and Dyes Inlets is approximately 252.3 km^2 (Johnston and others, 2009), and runoff enters the inlets through a series of small creeks with generally low flow. The major creeks that input to Sinclair Inlet are Gorst Creek at the head (no flow data available) and Blackjack Creek to the south (0.1–1.3 m^3/s), and the major inputs to Dyes Inlet are Chico Creek (0–11.7 m^3/s) and Clear Creek (0.1–4 m^3/s) (Albertson and others, 1993). Because the land use around the inlets is significantly urbanized, much of the runoff occurs via multiple stormwater combined sewer overflows (CSOs) and four wastewater treatment plants (WWTPs). Although peak flows from a single CSO or WWTP may be low compared to the creeks (peak of 1.5 m^3/s in 1994 at Bremerton WWTP), combined they can input as much freshwater as the creeks, and at times can provide highly localized input (Albertson and others, 1993).

Field Program

In 1994, three tripods supporting bottom-mounted, upward-facing Acoustic Doppler Current Profilers (ADCP) and conductivity/temperature/depth (CTD) recorders were deployed in the inlet for short periods during the late winter and summer seasons as part of a larger field program to determine contaminant transport patterns in the inlet (Gartner and others, 1998). The ADCPs and the CTDs were set to sample at 10 min intervals. Two tripods were deployed on each side of the shipyard at an East and a West site, and a third tripod was deployed in the middle of the inlet at a Center site (fig. 2). The water depths at these sites were 18, 13, and 14 m, respectively. A detailed description of the instrument and mooring setup is provided in Gartner and others (1998).

Wind velocity was measured every 15 min at one site, Quarry, at the head of the inlet and at another site, Marina, near the site of the Center mooring (fig. 2). The wind data at Quarry were collected over the full mooring deployment period (fig. 3). Wind data at Marina were collected over a shorter period. Winds discussed in this report use a coordinate system similar to that used for currents. Hence, both a northerly current and a northerly wind flows toward, not from, the north.

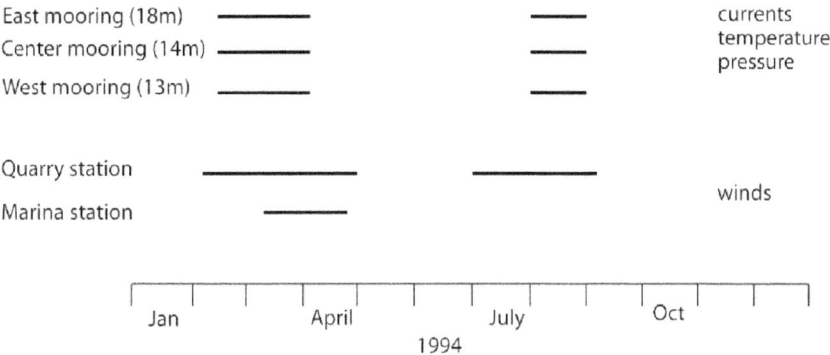

Figure 3. Timelines for measurements of currents, water temperature, pressure, and winds in Sinclair Inlet, Washington, 1994. The depths of the current moorings are shown in meters (m).

There are several small streams that supply fresh water to the inlet (fig. 1). Although daily discharge records from these streams generally are not available during the field program, a discharge record is available from a creek near Wauna, Washington (fig. 4), which is about 20 km south of Sinclair Inlet. The discharge patterns for this stream will be used in this report as a surrogate for the general discharge patterns in the watershed around Sinclair Inlet.

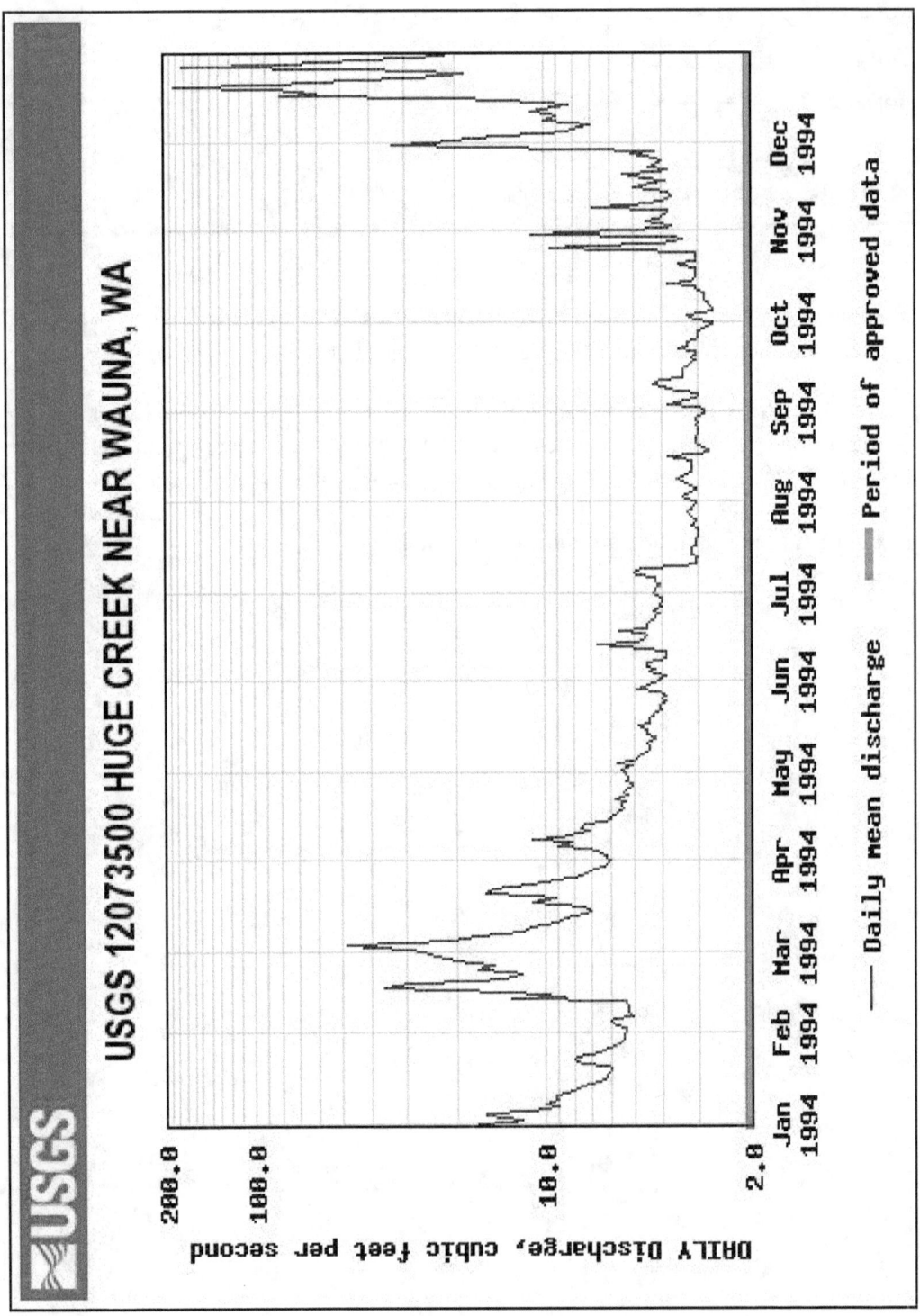

Figure 4. Graph showing daily discharge at Huge Creek about 20 km south of Sinclair Inlet near Wauna, Washinton, 1994.

6

Data Analyses

The datasets collected during the field program were passed through several quality-assurance control steps. The data were checked for errors because of instrument malfunction. These checks suggested that the salinity datasets were not reliable, as the measured salinity ranges were not consistent with CTD measurements taken during the deployment. Hence, the salinity datasets were discarded. Obvious measurement spikes were removed from the rest of the datasets. Greenwich mean time (GMT) was used as the common time base.

There were only short temporal gaps in the records of currents measured deeper than 6 m below the mean water level. Gaps in these records of less than 40 min were linearly interpolated. The few temporal gaps that lasted longer than 40 min, but less than 8 hours, were filled with a spectral method that uses the frequency properties of the adjacent data to fill the gap (Anderson, 1974). There were no gaps longer than 8 hours in these records.

Many more temporal gaps were found in records of current within 6 m of mean water level. If the gaps in a current record accounted for less than 10 percent of record length, the current record was included in the dataset analyzed in this report. If the gaps accounted for more than 10 percent of a record, which commonly happened for very near-surface currents, the record was discarded. Hence, the shallowest current discussed here were measured 3–4 m below the mean water in the inlet (table 1). Gaps of less than 8 hours in these shallow current records were filled as described above. Longer gaps were filled with data from the adjacent current measured either 0.5 or 1.0 m below the record under analysis. The resulting set of current records had no temporal gaps.

Station	Water Depth	Deepest current	Shallowest current	Vertical Resolution	Sampling frequency
	m	m	m	m	minutes
East_W	18.1	16.1	3.6	0.5	10
East_S	18.1	16.2	4.2	0.5	10
Center_W	14.1	11.9	2.9	1.0	10
Center_S	13.7	11.7	3.2	0.5	10
West_W	13.1	10.9	2.9	1.0	10
West_S	12.8	10.8	3.3	0.5	10

Table 1. Characteristics of the current datasets collected in the late winter (W) and summer (S) seasons in 1994 by Acoustic Doppler Current Profilers at the East, Center, and West stations in Sinclair Inlet, Washington. The water depth is relative to the mean water level and is based on the average pressure measured by the bottom-mounted pressure sensors. The depth of the deepest measured current is based on instrument characteristics and the measured water depth. The shallowest current depth is relative to mean water level.

All current records with a 0.5 m vertical resolution were averaged into 1 m bins. The currents were then averaged into a 1-hour sampling rate. The hourly currents were then lowpass filtered to remove fluctuations with periods less than 40 hours. These filtered datasets will be denoted as subtidal current records. All current records were then decomposed into along- and cross-inlet components, utilizing a rotation angle of 65 degrees. A positive along-inlet current flows toward the northeast, out of Sinclair Inlet. A positive cross-inlet current flows across the inlet toward the southeast. The lowpass-filtered, rotated set of current records was then trimmed to a common time period. The intervals for the 1994 winter and summer periods were February 20 (08:00) to April 2 (02:00) and July 31 (08:00) to August 27 (02:00), respectively.

The winds at the Quarry and Marina had similar structures. Both stations had fairly narrow ranges in wind direction; wind velocities were strongly aligned along an axis rotated 45 degrees clockwise from north, which is oriented approximately along the axis of Sinclair Inlet. The winds at both sites were decomposed into approximate along- and cross-inlet components using a rotation angle of 45 degrees. The along-inlet winds were much stronger than the cross-inlet winds at both sites (figs. 5 and 6). Both the amplitudes and frequency structures of the wind field were similar at the two sites. Because wind records at Quarry overlapped both winter and summer deployment periods, and records at Marina were shorter than the deployment periods, winds from Quarry are used to examine the wind-forced current patterns in the inlet.

The few gaps in the along- and cross-inlet winds at Quarry were filled with the spectral bridged methods described previously. The hourly observations of wind velocity at each site were converted to wind stress after the magnitude of the wind was adjusted to a height of 10 m above the land or sea surface using an empirical iteration scheme. The wind stress was then calculated using drag coefficient amplitude that varies with wind speed according to Wu (1980). Wind stress records were then lowpass filtered and trimmed to the same time periods as listed for currents.

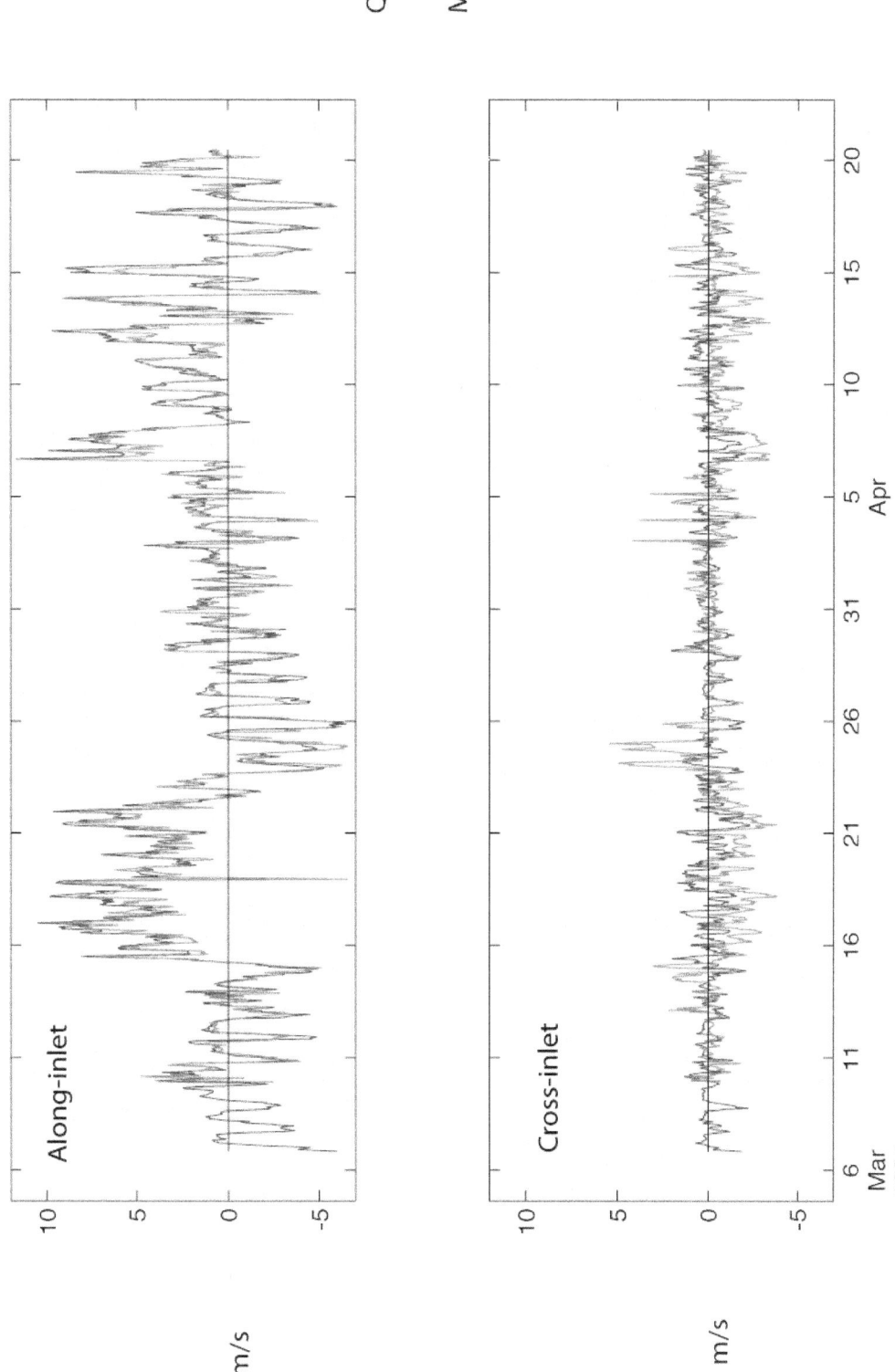

Figure 5. Graph showing hourly along- and cross-inlet wind speeds at the Quarry and Marina measurement stations during overlapping winter period in Sinclair Inlet, Washington. The positive along-inlet direction is 45 degrees. Units of wind speed are in meters per second.

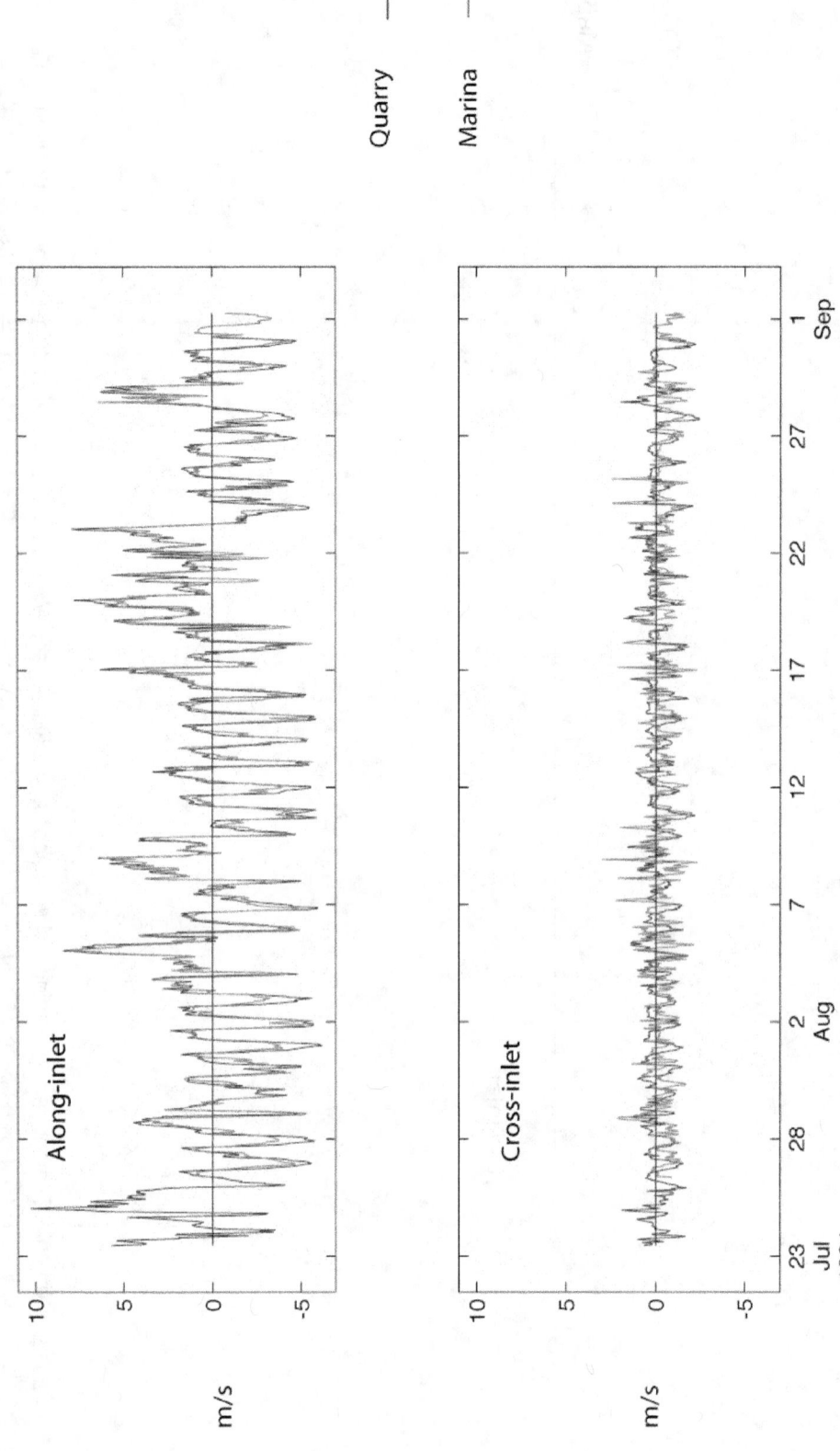

Figure 6. Graph showing hourly along- and cross-inlet wind speeds at the Quarry and Marina measurement sites during overlapping summer period in Sinclair Inlet, Washington. The positive along-inlet direction is 45 degrees. Units of wind speed are in meters per second.

10

Statistical Methods

Many of the analyses discussed in this report, which include calculations of means and variances of individual records together with the correlation and covariance amplitudes between joint datasets, use standard statistical methods. To be considered significant, all quantities must exceed the values for a standard error calculated at the 95-percent confidence level (Bendat and Piersol, 1986). The degrees of freedom, or the number of independent points, in an standard error calculation is based on the length of a record divided by its autocorrelation scale. For the subtidal datasets, there were 16.4 and 10.8 degrees of freedom in the winter and summer time periods, respectively.

In addition to these standard analyses, both real and complex Empirical Orthogonal Functions (EOF) were used to determine the correlated spatial and temporal structures in the current field (Kundu, and others, 1975; Joreskog and others, 1976; Priesendorfer, 1988). To insure that our calculation accounted for all components of the currents, we combined the along- and cross-inlet current components at each site into a covariance matrix that was used as the similarity matrix in the analysis. For a complex EOF, the along- and cross-inlet current components at each site are combined into a single complex vector, then the complex covariance matrix is calculated from the set of horizontal current records at each site. The individual modes in a particular EOF represent the vertical structure in the correlated portion of the set of currents in the analysis. Because the covariance matrix is the basis for the analysis, the most energetic currents at a particular depth or depth range tend to control the structure of the first mode.

Not all currents measured in the water column at a single station appear in the mode for that station. Currents at a particular depth are not considered part of a mode unless the correlation between the current and the time series for the mode is equal to or greater than the 95-percent confidence level for zero correlation. In these analyses, the amplitude of each site in the mode is specified in the spatial structure for the mode and the time series for each mode has unit variance. The amplitude is defined to be the square root of twice the portion of the current variance at a particular depth that is contained in the mode.

The currents in a complex mode have amplitudes that vary with depth, but stillhave a fixed orientation with respect to one another. However, the mode itself has an arbitrary overall orientation. Hence, the orientation of the major axis of the modal current is chosen to match that of a dominant current within the mode. For mode 1, the dominant current in the mode is the current measured about 5 m above the bed (tables 2). Hence, the orientation of the major axis of the first mode is aligned within that of the near-bed currents. The along-inlet orientation for the first mode is usually within 15 degrees of the axis of Sinclair Inlet. The exception is that modal currents at the West site in the winter season flow more across the inlet than do currents at the other two sites. A positive modal fluctuation indicates that currents flow toward the mouth of the inlet.

Station	Mode	Depth of current used for modal orientation	Modal orientation
		m	degrees
East_W	1	13	0
East_W	2	6	0
East_S	1	13	14
Center_W	1	9	-10
Center_S	1	9	0
West_W	1	8	35
West_W	2	10	35
West_S	1	8	16
West_S	2	5	18

Table 2. Orientation for complex current modes at East, Center and West sites, Sinclair Inlet, Washington. The modal time series have been aligned to the orientation of one of the strongest along-inlet currents within the mode. A positive modal orientation means the major axis of the modal current is rotated clockwise from the along-inlet direction of 65 degrees.

Moored Current Observations

Mean Current Flow Patterns

The few measurements we have of the mean flows in Sinclair Inlet suggest that the depth-averaged mean current tends to flow in a weak anticyclonic gyre around the upper portion of the inlet. The depth-averaged mean current flows across and slightly out the inlet on the eastern side of the mouth, and into the inlet near the Center site in both winter and summer seasons (table 3, figs. 7–9), with the strongest mean flows seen in winter. Farther into the estuary, at the western site, the depth-averaged mean current tends to flow into the inlet, similar to the trend seen at the center site. However, the strongest mean current at the western site is in the summer, not the winter, season.

Station	Along-inlet	error bar	Cross-inlet	error bar	Speed	Angle
	cm/s	cm/s	cm/s	cm/s	cm/s	degrees
East_W	**0.85**	0.77	**-1.02**	0.23	1.33	310
East_S	0.18	0.68	**-1.27**	0.26	1.28	278
Center_W	**-1.37**	0.49	0.35	0.39	1.41	164
Center_S	-0.19	0.55	0.20	0.23	0.28	130
West_W	-0.10	0.80	0.07	0.42	0.12	145
West_S	**-1.20**	0.52	**-0.42**	0.24	1.27	199

Table 3. The mean, depth-averaged currents in Sinclair Inlet, Washington. Positive along-inlet currents are directed out of the inlet. Positive cross-inlet currents are directed toward the southeast. Current amplitudes in bolded text are significant. Error bars are based on the temporal correlation scale of the subtidal currents (2.5 days) and are calculated at the 95-percent confidence level.

An examination of the vertical structure of the mean flows shows that the depth-averaged mean currents do not represent the dominant flow pattern in the estuary because the mean currents actually have significant vertical shears. The near-surface mean currents tend to flow out of the inlet (table 4, figs. 7–9). The mid-depth mean currents flow out of the inlet on the eastern side of the mouth, but flow into the inlet at the Center and West sites. The mean currents near the bed flow into the inlet at all sites.

Mean currents at the Eastern site

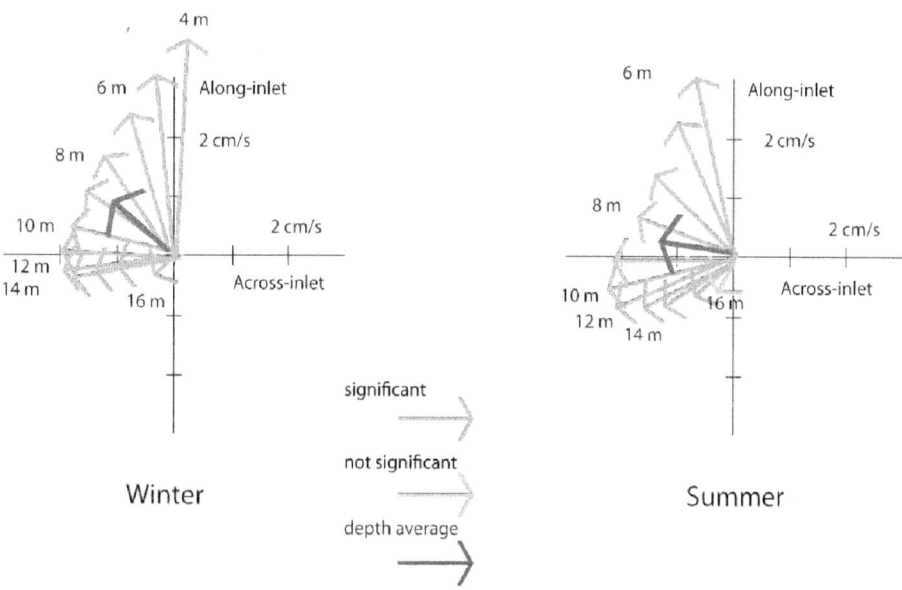

Figure 7. Graphs showing vertical structure of the mean currents at the East site in the winter and summer season in Sinclair Inlet, Washington. Positive along-inlet currents are directed out of the inlet. A green-colored arrow indicates that either the along- and/or the cross-inlet current is significant at the 95-percent confidence level. Blue indicates neither component of the mean currents is significant. A purple arrow represents the depth-averaged mean flow. The depth is meters below mean water level.

Mean currents at the center site

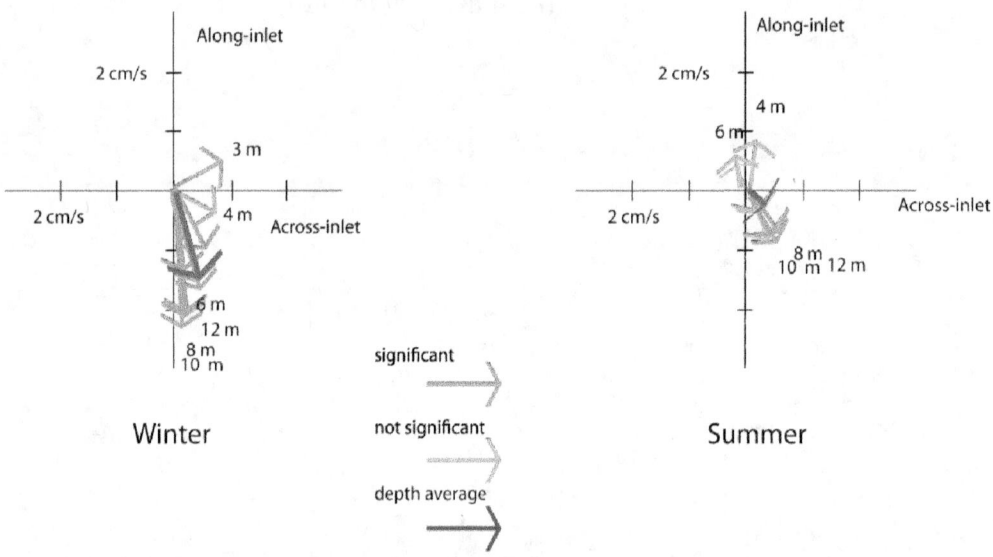

Figure 8. Graphs showing vertical structure of the mean currents at the Center site in the winter and summer season, Sinclair Inlet, Washington. Positive along-inlet currents are directed out of the inlet. A green-colored arrow indicates that either the along and/or the cross-inlet current is significant at the 95-percent confidence level. Blue indicates neither component of the mean currents is significant. A purple arrow represents the depth-averaged mean flow. The depth is meters below mean water level.

Mean currents at the Western site

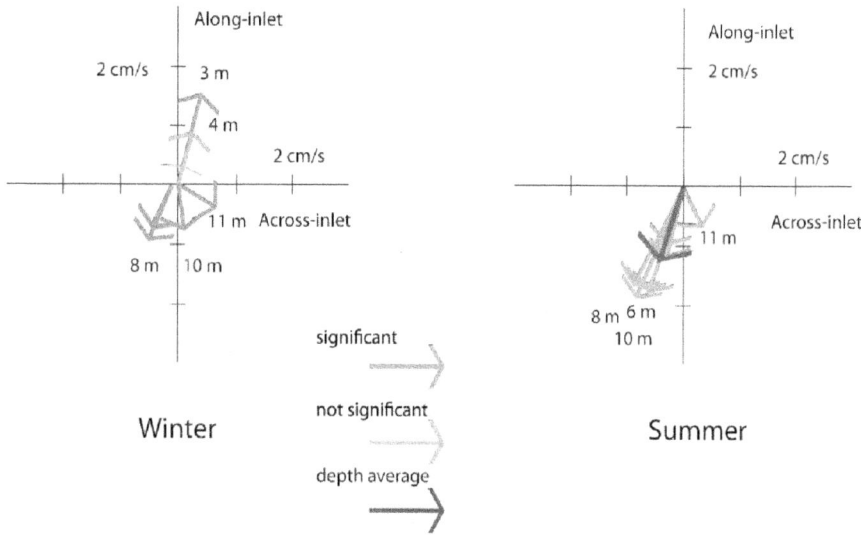

Figure 9. Graphs showing vertical structure of the mean currents in Sinclair Inlet at the western site in the winter and summer season. Positive along-inlet currents are directed out of the inlet. A green-colored arrow indicates that either the along and/or the cross-inlet current is significant at the 95-percent confidence level. Blue indicates neither component of the mean currents is significant. A purple arrow represents the depth-averaged mean flow. The depth is m below mean water level.

East_W					East_S			
Depth	Along-inlet	Error bar	Cross-inlet	Error bar	Depth	Along-inlet	Error bar	Cross-inlet	Error bar
m	cm/s	cm/s	cm/s	cm/s	m	cm/s	cm/s	cm/s	cm/s
3.9	**3.6**	0.7	0.2	0.4					
4.9	**3.1**	0.8	-0.3	0.3	4.9	**3.1**	0.9	**-0.7**	0.4
5.9	**2.3**	0.8	**-0.7**	0.3	5.9	**2.1**	0.9	**-1.0**	0.3
6.9	**1.6**	0.9	**-1.1**	0/3	6.9	**1.3**	0.9	**-1.4**	0.4
7.9	**1.0**	0.9	**-1.5**	0.4	7.9	0.6	0.9	**-1.7**	0.4
8.9	0.4	0.9	**-1.8**	0.4	8.9	0.1	0.8	**-1.9**	0.5
9.9	0.1	1.0	**-1.9**	0.4	9.9	-0.5	0.8	**-2.1**	0.5
10.9	-0.1	1.0	**-1.9**	0.4	10.9	**-0.8**	0.7	**-2.0**	0.5
11.9	-0.2	1.0	**-1.7**	0.4	11.9	**-0.9**	0.7	**-1.9**	0.4
12.9	-0.2	1.0	**-1.4**	0.4	12.9	**-0.9**	0.6	**-1.5**	0.3
13.9	-0.2	1.0	**-1.0**	0.4	13.9	**-0.8**	0.5	**-1.0**	0.3
14.9	-0.2	1.0	**-0.5**	0.4	14.9	**-0.7**	0.5	**-0.4**	0.3
15.9	-0.2	1.0	0.2	0.3	15.9	-0.5	0.5	0.3	0.3

Center_W					Center_S			
Depth	Along-inlet	Error bar	Cross-inlet	Error bar	Depth	Along-inlet	Error bar	Cross-inlet	Error bar
m	cm/s	cm/s	cm/s	cm/s	m	cm/s	cm/s	cm/s	cm/s
2.9	0.4	0.9	**0.8**	0.7					
3.9	-0.3	0.8	0.6	0.8	3.5	0.8	0.8	0.1	0.6
4.9	**-1.0**	0.8	0.5	0.7	4.5	0.6	0.7	-0.1	0.6
5.9	**-1.6**	0.8	0.4	0.7	5.5	0.3	0.7	-0.1	0.5
6.9	**-2.1**	0.7	0.2	0.6	6.5	-0.1	0.7	0.1	0.3
7.9	**-2.2**	0.8	0.1	0.4	7.5	-0.4	0.8	0.2	0.2
8.9	**-2.1**	0.9	0.1	0.3	8.5	-0.6	0.8	0.2	0.2
9.9	**-1.9**	0.9	0.2	0.2	9.5	-0.7	0.8	**0.3**	0.2
10.9	**-1.5**	0.9	**0.5**	0.2	10.5	**-0.8**	0.7	**0.5**	0.2
11.9	**-1.3**	0.8	**0.2**	0.2	11.5	**-0.8**	0.6	**0.6**	0.2

West_W					West_S			
Depth	Along-inlet	Error bar	Cross-inlet	Error bar	Depth	Along-inlet	Error bar	Cross-inlet	Error bar
m	cm/s	cm/s	cm/s	cm/s	m	cm/s	cm/s	cm/s	cm/s
2.9	**1.5**	1.4	0.4	0.6					
3.9	1.0	1.4	0.3	0.6	3.6	0.0	0.6	-0.1	0.4
4.9	0.4	1.3	0.1	0.7	4.6	**-1.0**	0.7	-0.3	0.4
5.9	-0.2	1.1	0.0	0.6	5.6	**-1.7**	0.6	**-0.6**	0.4
6.9	-0.7	0.9	-0.3	0.6	6.6	**-1.8**	0.6	**-0.8**	0.4
7.9	**-0.9**	0.7	-0.4	0.5	7.6	**-1.7**	0.6	**-0.9**	0.4
8.9	**-0.8**	0.5	-0.4	0.4	8.6	**-1.6**	0.6	**-0.7**	0.4
9.9	**-0.7**	0.4	0.1	0.3	9.6	**-1.2**	0.6	-0.3	0.4
10.9	**-0.4**	0.3	**0.7**	0.2	10.6	**-0.6**	0.5	0.3	0.5

Table 4. Amplitude of the mean current with depth in Sinclair Inlet. Positive along-estuary currents are directed out of the estuary. Positive cross-estuary currents are directed toward the southeast. Depths are the distance below mean water level. Bold current amplitudes are significant. Error bars are based on the temporal correlation scale of the subtidal currents (2.5 days) and are calculated at the 95-percent confidence level.

Tidal Current Flow Patterns

Most of the changes in sea level in Sinclair Inlet are caused by tidal fluctuations (fig. 10). The principal semidiurnal tidal oscillations, M_2, are a bit larger than 1 m at all measurement sites (table 5). The diurnal tidal amplitudes are smaller; K_1 fluctuations are about 0.75 m and O_1 fluctuations are about 0.5 m. Tidal fluctuations in the diurnal and semidiurnal bands account for 99 percent of the variance in sea level in the inlet. Sea-level fluctuations with periods longer than a few days (subtidal sea-level oscillations) are barely noticeable (less than 5 percent of the mean diurnal tidal range). The combined tidal fluctuations during the measurement period cause sea level to rise and decline over 4 m during spring tides. Because the mean depth of the inlet ranges from less than 10 m to about 20 m, this tidal range is a significant percentage of the total volume, thus signifying the importance of the tides to flushing in the estuary.

To evaluate the volumetric exchange caused by the tides, a simple mass balance was derived. If one considers the estuary to be a simple tetrahedron in shape extending from the head at Gorst Creek to the mouth at Rich Passage (at the south end of Bainbridge Island), the volume of the estuary is approximately 2.2×10^8 m^3. With a mean tide from mean low water to mean high water of 2.4 m (National Oceanic and Atmospheric Administration, 2012), this would result in a tidal prism of approximately 2.68×10^7 m^3, which is approximately one-tenth of the volume of the estuary. However, if one considers the estuary extending only to Port Bremerton at the mouth of Port Washington Narrows, the volume of the estuary is only 4.7×10^7 m^3 and the tidal prism is then 1.7×10^7 m^3, which is more than one-third of the volume of the estuary. Thus, assuming complete flushing (that is, only new water enters the estuary upon a new tide cycle), the upper estuary would theoretically flush in three tidal cycles. This is a very rough estimate of the volume of the estuary, however, and a more accurate estimate could be made using bathymetric data.

Station	O_1		K_1		M_2		S_2	
	Amp	Phase	Amp	Phase	Amp	Phase	Amp	Phase
	m		m		m		m	
East_W	0.49	255	0.64	287	1.08	17	0.32	47
East_S	0.51	260	0.78	301	1.13	17	0.31	53
Center_W	0.49	255	0.66	287	1.12	17	0.34	47
Center_S	0.51	262	0.77	302	1.12	20	0.30	57
West_W	0.48	255	0.64	287	1.08	18	0.33	47
West_S	0.50	261	0.77	301	1.10	17	0.30	54

Table 5. Tidal amplitudes from pressure measurements, Sinclair Inlet, Washington.

Consistent with the relatively large tidal changes in sea level, the tidal currents in Sinclair Inlet cause most of the fluctuations in the depth-averaged current records (fig. 10). The M_2 currents, which are the largest, are oriented primarily along the inlet and have amplitudes of 4–5 cm/s (table 4). The depth-averaged diurnal currents are smaller. They are oriented along the inlet and have amplitudes around 2 cm/s. The diurnal and semidiurnal tidal currents account for 60–85 percent of the total current variance in the inlet. The phase difference between the diurnal and semidiurnal currents and sea level is around 90 degrees.

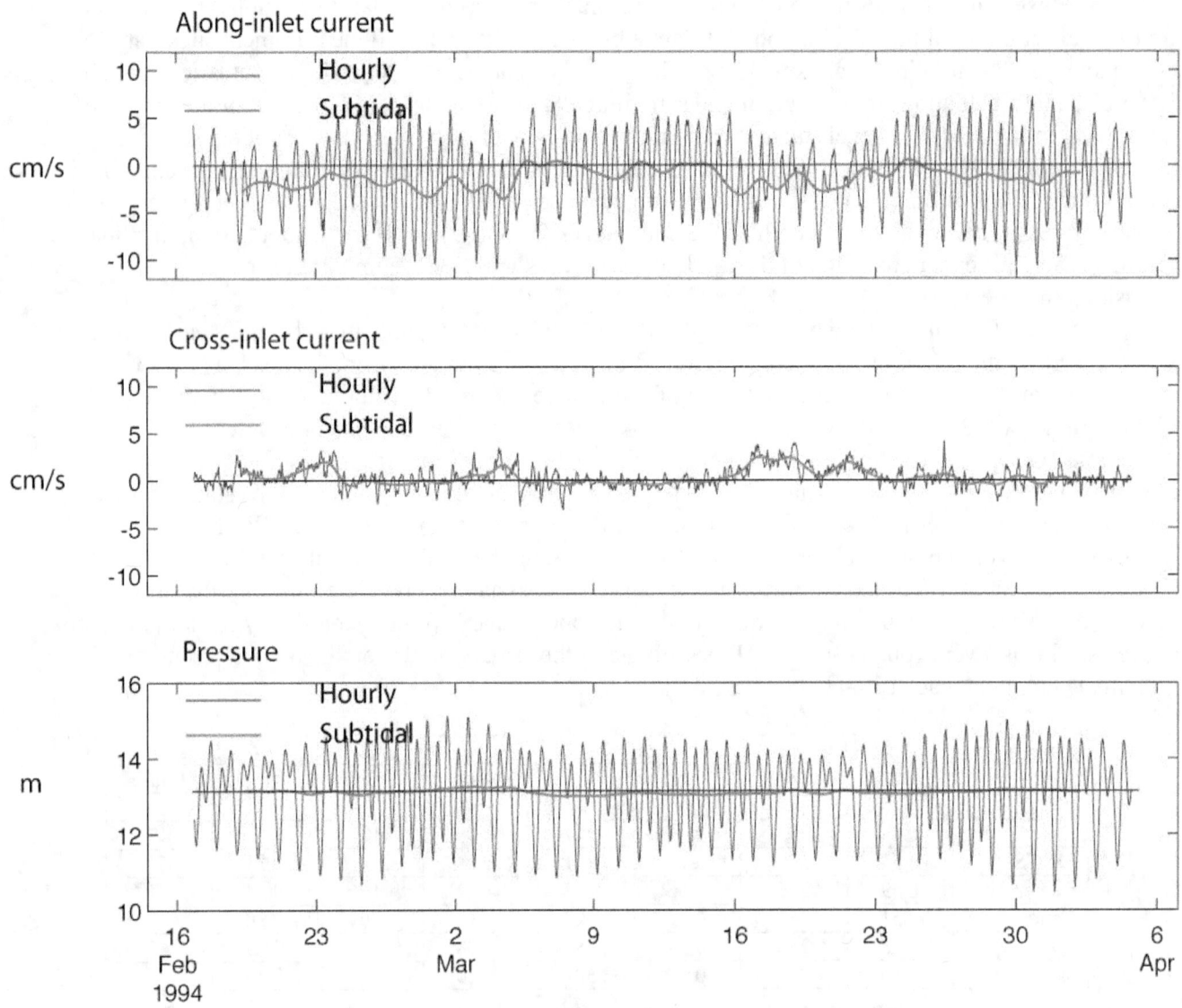

Figure 10. Graphs showing depth-averaged along and cross-inlet currents and sea level oscillations at the center site in Sinclair Inlet, Washington. Hourly (blue) and subtidal (red) records are depicted.

Even though there is some vertical shear in the tidal currents, the overall picture is that barotropic, or depth-averaged, currents are the dominant tidal currents in the inlet (tables 6, A1–A3). It is interesting to note that currents in the 24-hour tidal band are not surface-intensified, as they might be if the daily winds were driving strong currents. The diurnal currents have a fairly uniform amplitude and phase with depth. There is a slight suggestion that internal tides influence the vertical structure of the semidiurnal currents at the East site, but not at other sites in the inlet.

Station	O_1			K_1		
	Amplitude	Phase	Inc	Amplitude	Phase	Inc
	cm/s	degrees	degrees	cm/s	degrees	degrees
East_W	1.9	16	5	2.2	61	-1
East_S	2.6	352	-10	2.5	47	-1
Center_W	1.2	336	5	1.7	24	-3
Center_S	1.2	357	9	1.4	27	14
West_W	0.8	358	-22	1.2	243	-32
West_S	1.3	15	-18	1.3	87	-16
Pressure Current phase difference		101			114	
	M_2			S_2		
East_W	3.8	128	-21	1.3	150	-23
East_S	4.4	106	-20	1.2	149	-24
Center_W	4.6	116	1	1.4	143	-3
Center_S	4.7	115	7	1.4	150	2
West_W	3.4	110	-11	1.0	139	-17
West_S	3.8	117	-9	1.1	164	-14
Pressure Current phase difference		98			98	

Table 6. Graphs showing depth-averaged tidal current amplitudes, Sinclair Inlet, Washington. The inclination angle (Inc) is counterclockwise from the along-inlet direction (65 degrees). The phase difference between pressure and current also is reported.

Subtidal Current Flow Patterns

Vertical Flow Patterns

Oscillation patterns in the subtidal currents, which include the mean and longer period fluctuating portions of the flow field, reflect vertical structures measured in the mean flow patterns discussed previously (table 7). Fluctuations in subtidal currents near the bed are highly correlated at each of the three individual measurement sites. Table 7 shows that currents in neighboring bins 2–4 m near the bed are highly correlated to each other, (74–98 percent of the variance), demonstrating that near-bed currents have the same oscillation patterns in winter and summer seasons. This strong coupling between the near bed currents extends to more than 6 m above the bed, which is about one-third of the water column in this shallow inlet. The currents within 4–5 m of the surface share a similar high level of coupling, although this coupling does not tend to extend below the 5 m level. Hence, as might be expected, subtidal currents in the surface and near-bed layers are not usually correlated. Only the near-surface and near-bed currents at the Center site in winter have a significant, albeit negative, correlation.

Station	Current depth 1	Current depth 2	Amplitude
	m	m	
East_W			
	3.9	4.9	0.83
	3.9	5.9	NS
	3.9	15.9	NS
	13.9	15.9	0.98
	14.9	15.9	0.99
East_S			
	4.9	5.9	0.97
	4.9	6.9	0.91
	4.9	15.9	NS
	13.9	15.9	0.87
	14.9	15.9	0.95
Center_W			
	2.9	3.9	0.92
	2.9	4.9	NS
	2.9	11.9	-0.69
	9.9	11.9	0.96
	10.9	11.9	0.98
Center_S			
	3.5	4.5	0.83
	3.5	5.5	NS
	3.5	11.5	NS
	9.5	11.5	0.85
	10.5	11.5	0.94
West_W			
	2.9	3.9	0.97
	2.9	4.9	0.94
	2.9	10.9	NS
	8.9	10.9	0.62
	9.9	10.9	0.86
West_S			
	3.6	4.6	0.84
	3.6	5.6	0.63
	3.6	10.6	NS
	8.6	10.6	0.84
	9.6	10.6	0.95

Table 7. Correlations (r) between different pairs of along-inlet subtidal current bins at each station. The depths of currents in each pair are measured in meters below mean sea level. The zero correlation levels for winter and summer are 0.49 and 0.61, respectively. NS indicates that the correlation not significant.

Although these individual flow patterns are noteworthy, it is difficult to determine a robust flow pattern for the inlet from comparisons among paired sets of relatively short current records. A complex modal analysis highlights the spatial patterns of the fluctuations in an entire set of current records that are correlated. The first mode usually accounted for over three-quarters of the subtidal current variance at a given site. Hence, it represents the dominant vertical structure in the subtidal current pattern.

The first mode at the eastern site shows that in winter, the mid-level and near-bed currents dominate the subtidal fluctuations (fig. 11). The near-surface currents are insignificant. Currents in the first mode are strong enough, with speeds of 2–3 cm/s, to reinforce, and even reverse, the mean flow over the middle and deeper portions of the water column (table 8, figs. 12–13). Hence the deeper, measured currents at the eastern site flow in and out of the inlet. Note that mode 2 accounts for more than 50 percent of the wintertime fluctuations in the very near-surface currents at the eastern site and are therefore uncoupled from the mid-depth and near-bed flows. This suggests that some of the processes that force the near-surface currents do not affect the mid-depth or near-bed flows. Hence, near-surface currents can flow more strongly out of the inlet, independent of deeper flow patterns.

Site	Site	Correlation amplitude	Lag
			Hours
Depth-Averaged Current			
East_W	Center_W	0.78	0
East_W	West_W	-0.58	- 12
Center_W	West_W	-0.49	-12
East_S	Center_S	NS	--
East_S	West_S	NS	--
Center_S	West_S	NS	--
Surface currents at 4 m			
East_W	Center_W	0.56	-12
East_W	West_W	NS	--
Center_W	West_W	0.58	0
East_S	Center_S	NS	--
East_S	West_S	NS	--
Center_S	West_S	NS	--
Near-bed currents at 10 m			
East_W	Center_W	0.77	0
East_W	West_W	NS	--
Center_W	West_W	-0.55	-12
East_S	Center_S	NS	--
East_S	West_S	NS	--
Center_S	West_S	NS	--
Mode 1 currents			
East_W	Center_W	0.82	0
East_W	West_W	-0.71	0
Center_W	West_W	-0.88	0
East_S	Center_S	MG (0.60)	--
East_S	West_S	NS	--
Center_S	West_S	-0.65	0

Table 8. Correlations (r) between along-inlet subtidal currents different locations. The zero correlation levels for winter and summer are 0.49 and 0.61, respectively. NS indicates that the correlation is not significant. MG indicates that the correlation is marginal. A negative lag indicates that the first site in a pair leads the second. A lag of less than 10 hours is not significant.

Structure of subtidal modal currents at the Eastern site

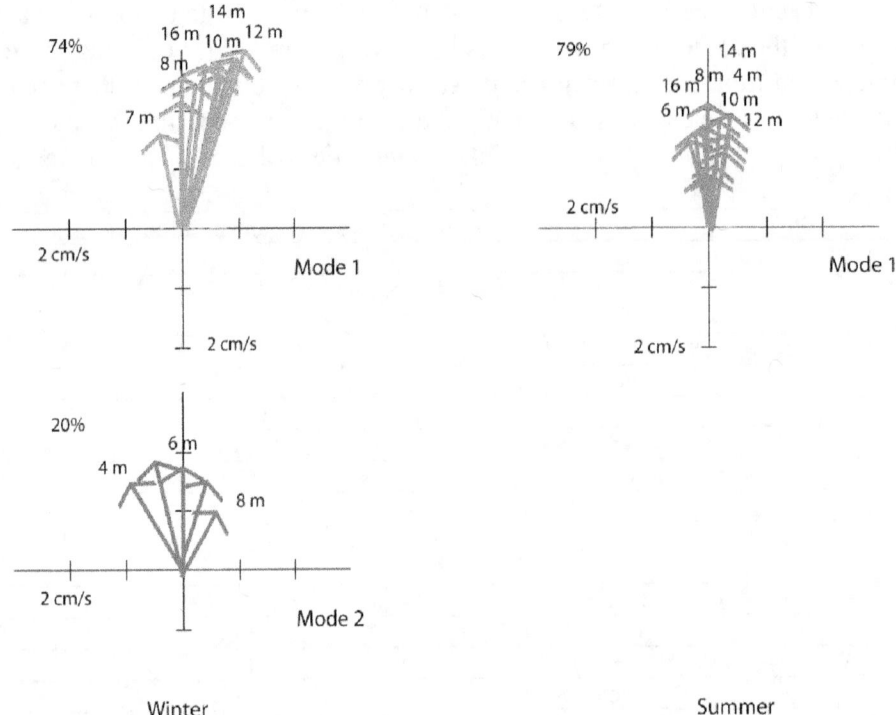

Figure 11. Graphs showing amplitudes of subtidal currents in the first and second modes for the eastern site. The percentage of the current variance the mode accounts for is noted next to the modal structure. The depth in meters of the measured currents in the mode are noted in the figures. The orientation of the currents in the mode are fixed relative to each other. Positive current fluctuations are directed out of the inlet.

Subtidal and Mode 1 wintertime currents at the Eastern site.

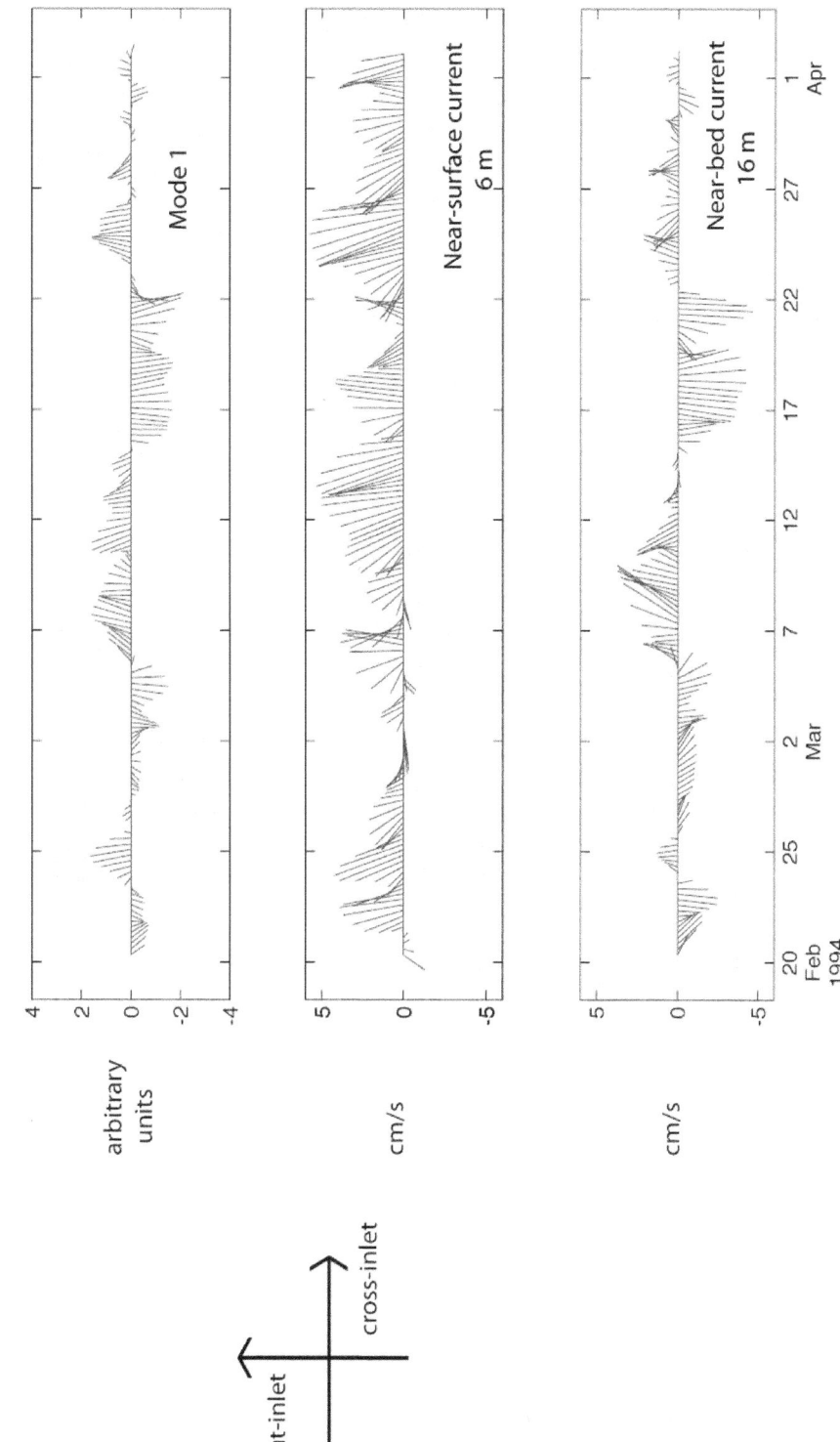

Figure 12. Vector plots of subtidal and mode 1 wintertime currents at the eastern site in Sinclair Inlet. A vertical (horizontal) line denotes currents are flowing out of (across) the inlet.

23

Subtidal and Mode 1 summertime currents at the Eastern site.

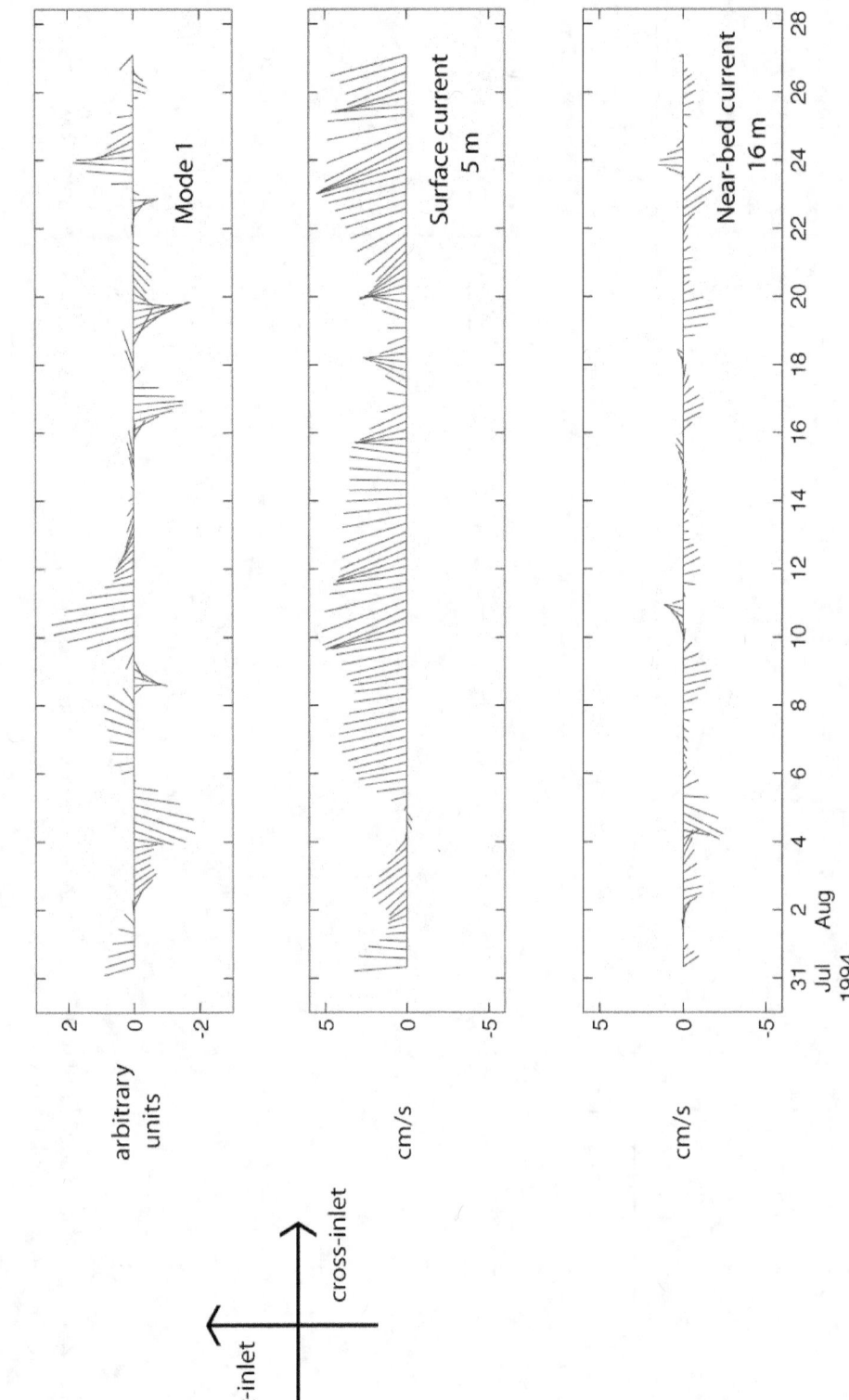

Figure 13. Vector plots of subtidal and mode 1 summertime currents at the eastern site in Sinclair Inlet. A vertical (horizontal) line denotes currents are flowing out of (across) the inlet.

24

The first mode at the center site accounts for more than 70 percent of the current variance in both seasons, showing subtidal current fluctuations are strongly correlated across the entire water column in the middle of the inlet (fig. 14). Even though the near-surface currents are strong and coupled with the deeper currents at this site, the direction of currents at each level varies rapidly with depth. The near-surface currents flow toward the head or across the inlet when near-bed currents flow toward the mouth. Fluctuation amplitudes are 2–3 cm/s over the entire water column in winter and somewhat smaller in the summer. Even though the mean currents over the mid and lower portions of the water column flow strongly into the inlet, the measured mid-level and near-bed subtidal currents at the center site often oppose each other, with the near-bed currents typically flowing out of the inlet (figs. 15–16).

At the western site, the first winter mode contains about 90 percent of the current variance and is dominated by the surface and mid-depth flow (fig. 17), contrary to the pattern seen at the eastern site (fig. 11). The near-bed currents are weak and barely correlated with the stronger surface flows (fig. 18). Because the winter mean flow also has a strong vertical shear, the surface and near-bed currents flow in opposite directions and have different temporal patterns. A similar sheared flow pattern is found in the summer period, except that in this season it is the near-surface currents that are uncorrelated with flow over the rest of the water column (figs. 13, 16, and 19).

Structure of subtidal modal currents at the Center site

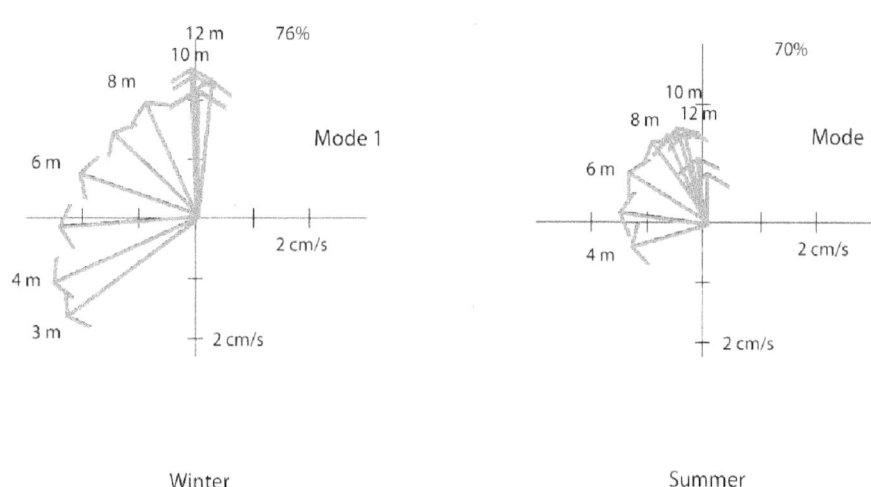

Winter   Summer

Figure 14. Graphs showing amplitudes of subtidal currents in the first and second modes for the center site. The percentage of the current variance the mode accounts for is noted next to the modal structure. The depth in meters of the measured currents in the mode are noted in the figures. The orientation of the currents in the mode are fixed relative to each other. Positive current fluctuations are directed out of the inlet.

Subtidal and Mode 1 wintertime currents at the Center site.

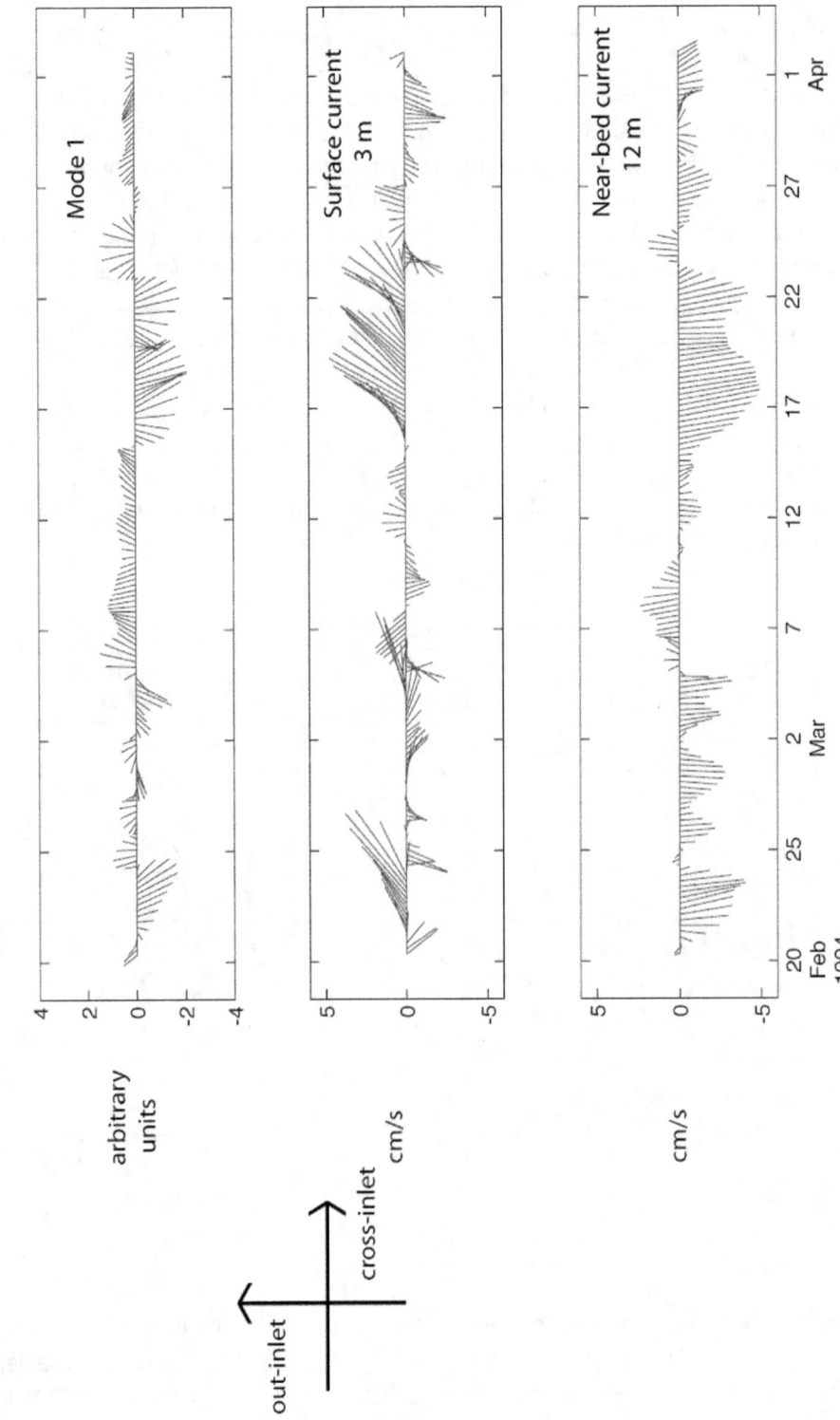

Figure 15. Vector plots of subtidal and mode 1 wintertime currents at the center site in Sinclair Inlet. A vertical (horizontal) line denotes currents are flowing out of (across) the inlet.

26

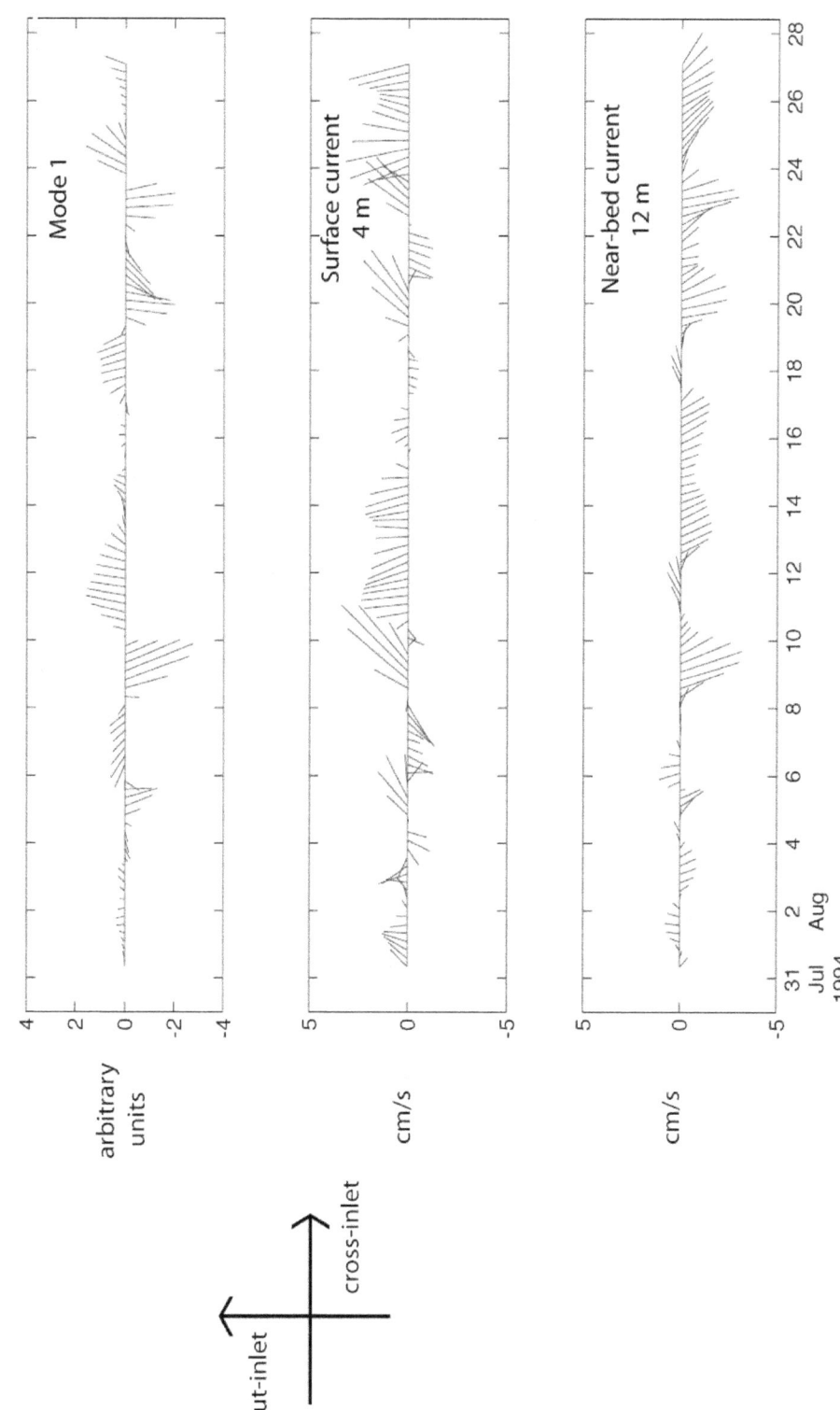

Figure 16. Vector plots of subtidal and mode 1 summertime currents at the eastern center site in Sinclair Inlet. A vertical (horizontal) line denotes currents are flowing out of (across) the inlet.

Structure of subtidal modal currents at the Western site

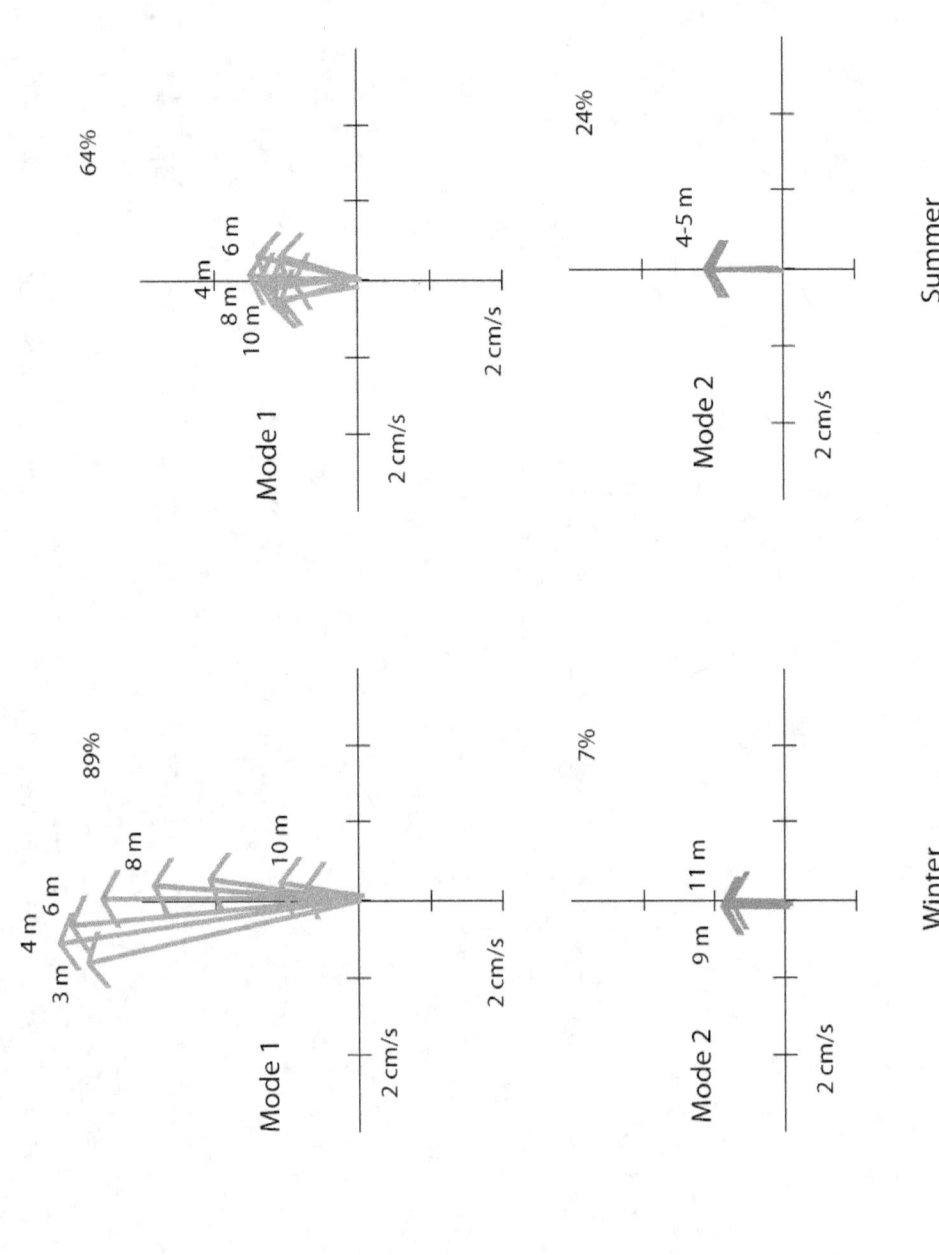

Figure 17. Graphs showing amplitudes of subtidal currents in the first and second modes for the western site. The percentage of the current variance the mode accounts for is noted next to the modal structure. The depth in meters of the measured currents in the mode are noted in the figures. The orientation of the currents in the mode are fixed relative to each other. Positive current fluctuations are directed out of the inlet.

28

Subtidal and Mode 1 wintertime currents at the Western site.

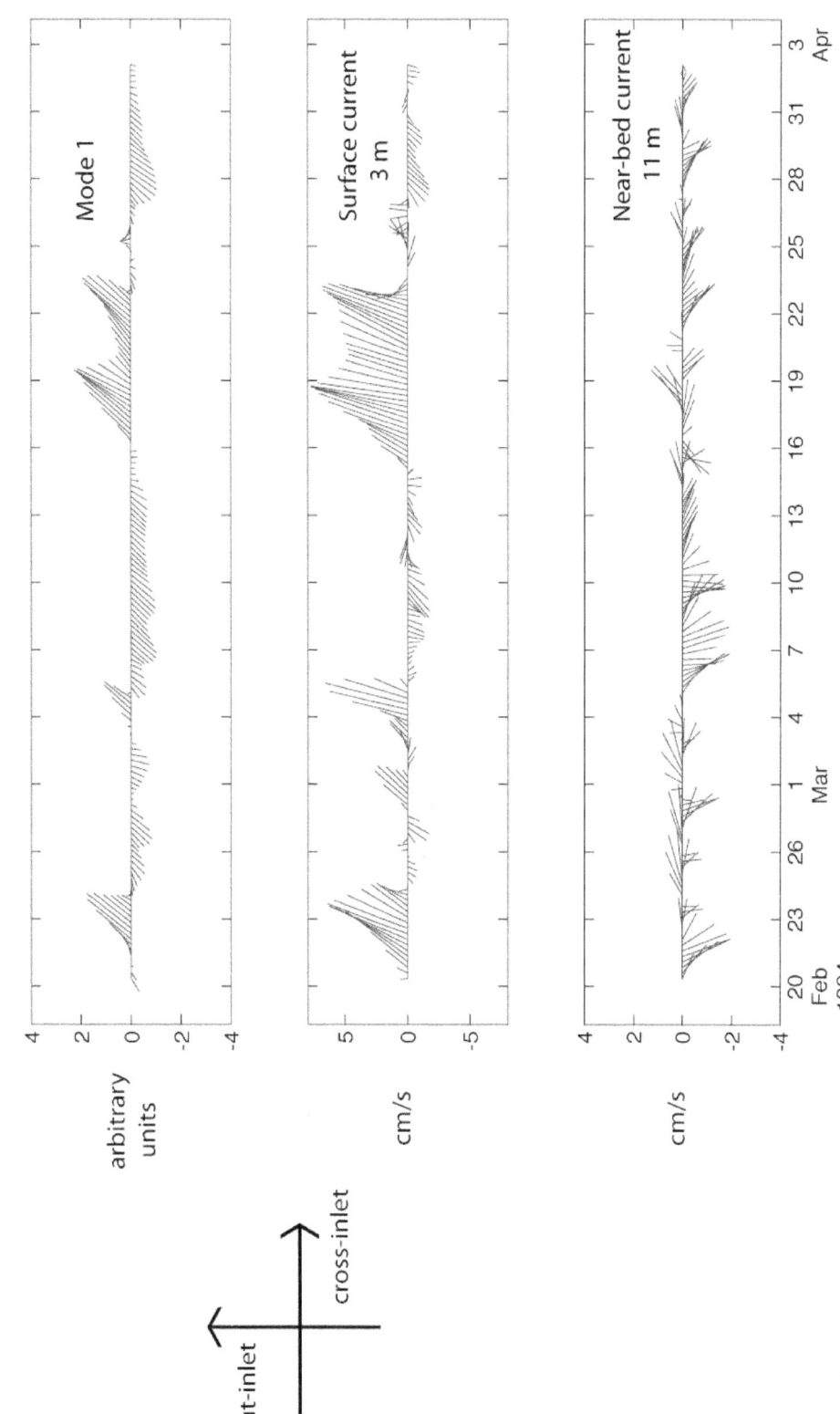

Figure 18. Vector plots of subtidal and mode 1 winter currents at the western site in Sinclair Inlet. A vertical (horizontal) line denotes currents are flowing out of (across) the inlet.

Subtidal and Mode 1 summer time currents at the Western site.

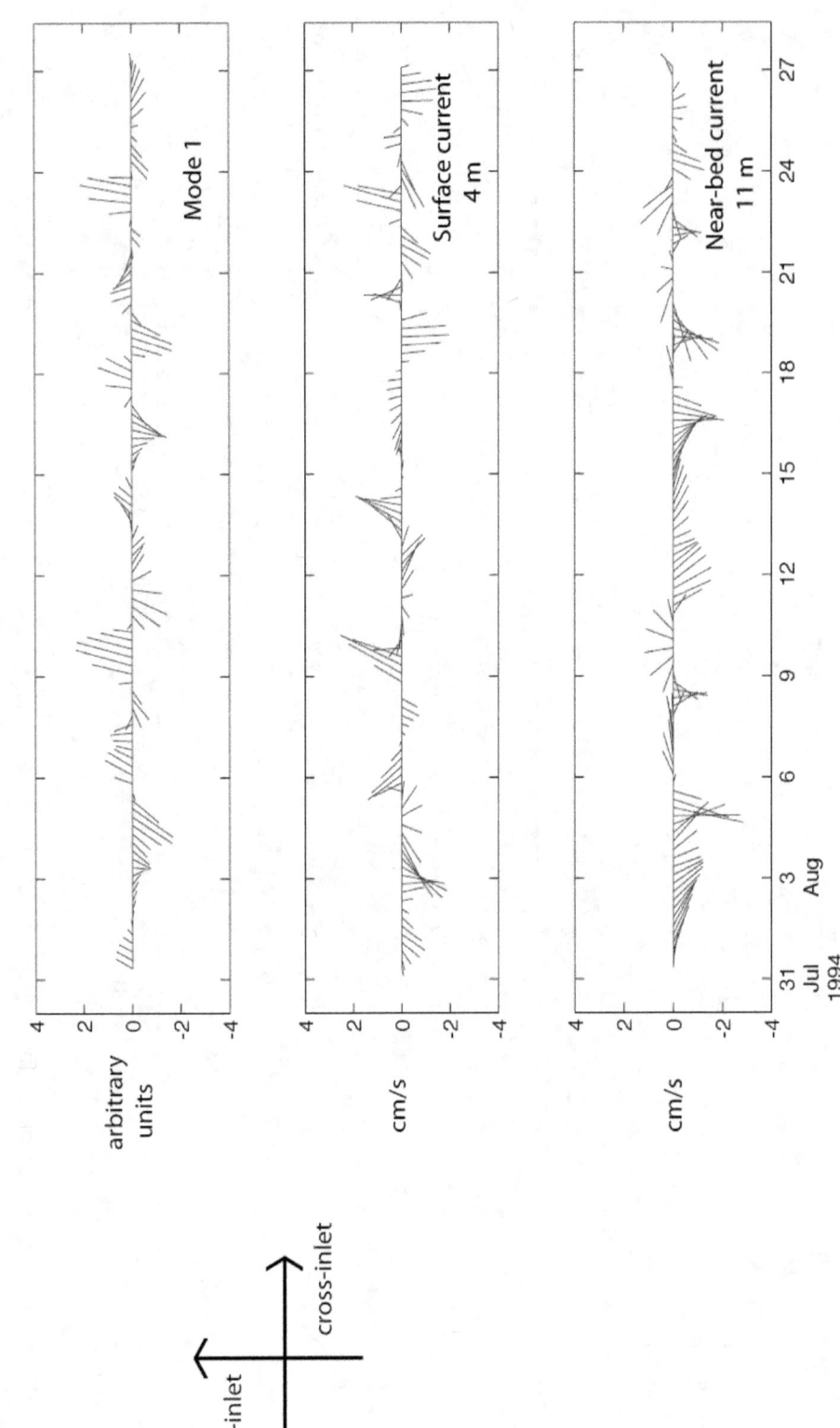

Figure 19. Vector plots of subtidal and mode 1 summer currents at western site in Sinclair Inlet. A vertical (horizontal) line denotes currents are flowing out of (across) the inlet.

30

Horizontal Flow Patterns

There are strong, measurable opposing flows in the horizontal spatial pattern of subtidal currents in winter in the Sinclair Inlet (table 8). Flow pattern in the summer cannot be determined because the summer current records are shorter than winter records. The winter depth-averaged, along-inlet currents at the mouth (East site) and in the center of the inlet tend to flow together in and out of the inlet (table 8). Fluctuations toward the mouth of the inlet may reduce or overpower the depth-averaged mean flow into the inlet at the center site. The depth-averaged, along-inlet currents farther into the inlet, at the western site, oppose these flows and flow more strongly into the inlet when currents at the mouth flow out.

The near-surface, along-inlet currents are more positively correlated than the depth-averaged currents. Near-surface subtidal currents tend to flow together (with some exceptions), toward or away from the inlet mouth, at all sites (table 8). The winter near-bed currents flow in the same direction only at sites near the center and mouth of the inlet, similar to the depth-averaged flow pattern.

Correlations among modal currents reflect those of the depth-averaged currents. The first mode at the eastern site, which is dominated by the mid-level and near-bed currents, is positively correlated with the center site (table 8). Given that the center mode is strongly sheared, this correlation suggests that when mid-level and near-bed currents at the mouth of the inlet flow strongly into the inlet, fluctuations in the mid-depth and near-bed currents at the center site also flow into the inlet, reinforcing the tendency of the mean flow at these depths to carry water into the inlet. The near-surface currents at the center site tend to flow in the opposite direction of the near-bed currents at both sites. Hence, inflow at the bed is associated with outflow at the surface. This coherent, sheared flow pattern supports the relationships previously discussed between individual pairs of currents. The near-bed currents at both sites (east and center) are positively correlated. The near-surface currents at the eastern site, which are independent from the mid-level currents, are positively correlated with near-surface currents at the center site.

Contrary to modal structures of currents at the mouth and center of the inlet, the first mode currents at the western site, which is farthest into the inlet, are dominated by near-surface currents. This western mode is strongly negatively correlated with the first modes at both the center and eastern sites (table 8). Hence, the near-surface currents at the western site flow out of the inlet when near-bed currents at the center and eastern sites flow in. This pattern supports the inference that the near-surface currents move together, and opposite to the near-bed currents, in and out of the inlet.

Even though the structure of the flow pattern in the Sinclair Inlet can be classified into a loose regional pattern, it is not comprehensive or stable. The subtidal currents have complex, fairly short spatial scales that vary with depth in the inlet. The pattern, which is derived from time-limited datasets collected primarily in the winter season, could change with time if the force that controls that circulation pattern changes. Even the general pattern described previously does not account for the total current field in the inlet. For example, measurements suggest the near-bed currents are divergent between the mouth and head of the inlet. The correlation amplitudes imply that at least 50 percent of the energy in this current field is not homogeneous across the estuary (table 8). Similarly, a lot of the energy in the near-surface currents is spatially uncorrelated.

Forcing of Subtidal Currents in Sinclair Inlet

Wind-Forced Currents

In general, the measurement periods were too short to determine whether a robust wind-driven current pattern is common in Sinclair Inlet. The winds, which would need to account for more than 25–45 percent of the energy in the subtidal current field before a relationship between winds and currents could be deemed robust, were not always correlated with individual current records. However, there were a few significant wind-current coupling patterns. Along-inlet wind stress was positively correlated with near-surface currents at the western site and nearly significantly correlated with surface currents at the center site (table 9). It was negatively correlated with near-bed currents at these same two sites. Hence, a 1 dyne/cm^2 along-inlet wind stress could drive a 3–9 cm/s near-surface current out of the inlet and a 6 cm/s near-bed current back into the inlet at the east and center sites.

Correlations between wind stress and the modal currents support the suggestion that positive, along-inlet winds drive surface currents out and near-bed currents back into the inlet. In winter, about 60 percent of the energy in the western mode, which is dominated by surface currents, is positively correlated with wind stress (table 9). More than 70 percent of the energy in the modal currents at the east and center sites, which represents mid-level and near-bed currents, is negatively correlated with wind stress. The pattern was similar in the summer season.

Wind Stress	Current site	Correlation amplitude	Lag	Slope	Intercept
			Hours	cm/s per dynes/cm**2	cm/s
Surface currents at 4 m					
Quarry_W	East_W	NS			
Quarry_W	Center_W	MG(0.48)	0	3.3	-0.7
Quarry_W	West_W	0.79	0	8.9	-0.2
Quary_S	East_S	NS	--	--	--
Quarry_S	Center_S	NS	--	--	--
Quarry_S	West_S	NS	--	--	--
Near-bed currents at 10 m					
Quarry_W	East_W	-0.83	0	-6.6	0.9
Quarry_W	Center_W	-0.83	0	-6.3	-1.1
Quarry_W	West_W	NS	--	--	--
Quary_S	East_S	NS	--	--	--
Quarry_S	Center_S	-0.68	0	-5.5	-0.8
Quarry_S	West_S	NS			
Mode 1 current					
Quarry_W	East_W	-0.85	0	--	--
Quarry_W	Center_W	-0.87	0	--	--
Quarry_W	West_W	0.78	0	--	--
Quary_S	East_S	-0.75	0	--	--
Quarry_S	Center_S	-0.81	0	--	--
Quarry_S	West_S	NS	--	--	--

Table 9. Corrlelations (r) between along-inlet wind stress and along-inlet currents in Sinclair Inlet. In the winter and summer periods, the zero correlation level is 0.49 and 0.61, respectively. NS indicates that the correlation amplitude is below significance levels. MG indicates that the correlation amplitude is marginal. A negative lag indicates that the first site in a pair leads the second. A lag of less than 10 hours is not significant.

Riverine Influence

Inputs of fresh water through river discharge have the potential to affect subtidal exchange patterns in Sinclair Inlet., Data from the moorings deployed in this program did not provide a reliable measurement of salinity along the inlet either at the surface or near the bed. Hence, we cannot determine either the vertical or horizontal stratification of the water column or changes in that stratification. The streamflow data suggests that fresh-water inflow into the inlet may be an important mechanism for forcing exchange in the inlet, especially in winter (fig. 4). However, the relative strength of that forcing cannot be determined from this particular dataset. Previous studies have shown that salinity does not vary greatly over the course of the year in the inlet, and ephemeral nature of freshwater input suggests that the riverine influence is small and short lived. The greatest degree of stratification tends to occur in summer months, primarily because of thermal stratification. Nevertheless, this thermal stratification is not constant in summer, and the water column can mix and break down (Albertson and others, 1993).

Discussion

The most prominent fluctuations in sea level and currents in Sinclair Inlet are caused by tides. The tidal range in sea level, up to 4 m, is about one-quarter of the water depth. The tidal currents associated with these sea-level oscillations typically have an 8 cm/s amplitude that is uniform with depth. Hence, large volumes of water and material suspended across the entire water column move in and out of in the inlet once or twice a day. The excursion length for this exchange is about 1.7 km, based on a typical 8 cm/s tidal current and a duration of 6 hours (from slack ebb to slack flood). The net exchange caused by these large fluctuations depends, in part, on (1) the mixing within the inlet caused by the large tides and (2) by the strength of the currents that flow past the mouth of the inlet, either from Dyes Inlet or from the Port Orchard channel. If processes outside the mouth of Sinclair Inlet cause the water and suspended materials leaving the inlet to be removed from the system before the tides carry them back into the inlet, the net exchange caused by tidal processes would be significantly enhanced.

The phase difference between the tidal currents and sea level is about 100 degrees. The sign of the phase difference indicates that tidal currents enter the inlet as sea level rises and leave the inlet as sea level declines. Hence, the depth-averaged tides in the inlet can be modeled primarily as a simple standing wave.

The vertical shear in the Sinclair Inlet exchange patterns are primarily associated with the subtidal, rather than the tidal, flows because subtidal currents tend to change direction and/or amplitude with depth. The subtidal currents, which are smaller than tidal currents, tend to be opposite in direction between the surface and the near-bed for periods of several days. Even a small shear of 4 cm/s over a period of 3 days can cause the distance that surface and near-bottom waters are transported to differ by 10 km, a distance that is longer than the length of the inlet. The patterns in the subtidal-flow field suggest surface currents tend to move out of the inlet, while near-bed currents move into the inlet (fig. 16). The structures in the mean flow support this observation, in that mean near-surface flows tend to be out of the inlet, while near-bed flow move water into the inlet. This is not exclusively true, however, as the mean patterns from the western site in summer demonstrate (fig. 9).

One reason for the sheared flow pattern in subtidal, but not tidal, currents is that winds are effective at forcing currents only when they have a constant direction for periods of 3 days or more. The strong, daily cycle in wind stress does not drive significant currents in the inlet. However, when the average wind stress blows along and out of the inlet for period of several days, surface currents tend to leave the inlet, while near-bed currents enter the inlet. Given the longer period that wind amplitudes range between 0.3 and 0.8 dynes/cm^2, this drives a 2–5 cm/s current into, or out of, the inlet. Over a period of 3–5 days, the transport in the surface or near-bed layer ranges between 5 and 20 km, distances that easily encompass the length of the estuary. Given that the wind stress in the winter season tends to flow out of the estuary, there is a slight tendency for the wind-driven, near-bed currents to carry water into the inlet. There is more fluctuation in the near-surface flows in summer. An estimate of the net wind-driven transport in the surface and bottom layers is problematical, as error bars are large and instruments in the two deployments did not measure the currents within a few meters of the surface or the bed.

It is uncertain whether riverine flow enhances the tendency for surface waters to flow out of, and bottom waters to flow into, the estuary during the winter. The river discharge data from nearby streams suggest that fresh-water input could force a sheared flow pattern, but there is no reliable salinity data to support this inference. The small amount of salinity data collected in other measurement programs (Albertson, 1993) suggests that both the horizontal and vertical salinity stratification within the estuary is minimal at certain times of the year. Hence, riverine influences on the flow in the inlet may beinsignificant, or limited to a few months of the year. More data are needed before one can evaluate riverine influences.

Conclusions

It is clear that several processes influence the circulation and exchange patterns in Sinclair Inlet. Tidal currents dominated the flow and caused currents to flow uniformly into and out of the inlet over periods of 6–12 hours. The flow pattern does not have significant shear for periods longer than several days. Subtidal near-surface currents tended to flow out of, and near-bed currents back into, the inlet. There was a tendency for winds, which blow along and out of the estuary in winter, to induce a sheared exchange pattern in the inlet.

This measurement program was originally focused on erosion and transport of bed sediment as a result of tides and waves, and not the overall exchange patterns. Thus, the datasets collected in this program were too limited in scope and time to allow the development of a robust estimate of the characteristics of the many processes that drive exchange between the Sinclair Inlet and the waters in Puget Sound. Nevertheless, the data suggest that surface waters tend to leave the inlet, while near-bed currents tend to enter it. The length of the dataset does not allow for the dominant processes that control exchange into and out of the inlet to be clearly identified. Longer measurement periods of local currents, wind stress, temperature, and salinity at many stations in the inlet need to be collected before stable exchange patterns can be verified. In particular, given that (1) the topographic setting of the inlet is complex; (2) human influences on the inlet are extensive; and (3) the spatial scales of flow patterns are short, it is probable that a 3-dimensional numerical model calibrated by an extensive measurement program needs to be developed before robust estimates of exchange patterns can be developed for the Sinclair Inlet.

Acknowledgments

The data analyzed in this report were collected 1994 by a consortium of researchers from the U.S. Geological Survey (USGS). A full description of the program, the data sources, the support and the researchers involved is given in Gartner and others(1998). Support for the reanalysis of the data was provided by the U.S. Geological Survey and the U.S. Navy. The authors would like to thank Jessica Lacy and Jonathan Warrick of the USGS Coastal and Marine Geology program for their helpful comments that greatly improved this report.

References Cited

Albertson, S.L, Newton, J. Eisner, L., Janzen, C., and Bell, S., 1993, 1992 Sinclair and Dyes Inlet seasonal monitoring report: State of Washington Department of Ecology, 91 p., accessed February 26, 2013, at http://www.ecy.wa.gov/biblio/95345.html.

Anderson, N.O., 1974, On the calculation of filter coefficients for maximum entropy spectral analysis: Geophysics, v. 39, p. 69–72.

Bendat, J.S., and Piersol, A.G., 1986, Random data—analysis and measurement procedures (2d ed.): New York, Wiley-Interscience, 566 p.

Finlayson, D., 2005, The geomorphology of Puget Sound beaches: School of Oceanography, University of Washington, Seattle, Washington, Ph.D. dissertation.

Gartner, J.W., Prych, E.A., Tate, G.B., Cacchione, D.A., Cheng, R.T., Bidlake, W.R., and Ferreira, J.T., 1998, Water velocities and the potential for the movement of bed sediments in Sinclair Inlet of Puget Sound, Washington: U.S. Geological Survey Open-File Report 98-572, 140 p.

Johnston, R.K, Wang, P.F., Loy, E.C., Blake, A.C., Richter, K.E., Brand, M.C., Kyburg, C.E., Skahill, B.E., May, C.W., Culinan, V. Choi, W., Whitney, V.S., Leisle, D.E., Beckwith, B., 2009, An integrated watershed and receiving water model for fecal coliform fate and transport in Sinclair and Dyes Inlets, Puget Sound, Washington: Space and Navel Warfare Systems Center, Technical Report 1977, 151 p.

Joreskog, K.G., Klovan, J.E., and Reyment, R.A., 1976, Geological factor analysis: New York, Elsevier, 178 p.

Kundu, P.K., Allen, J.S., and Smith, R.L., 1975, Modal decomposition of the velocity field near the Oregon coast: Journal of Geophysical Oceanography, v. 5, p. 683–704.

National Oceanic and Atmospheric Aadministration (NOAA), National ocean service tidal station datum for Port Bremerton, Washington: NOAA database, accessed February 26, 2012, at *http://tidesandcurrents.noaa.gov/data_menu.shtml?stn=9445958%20Bremerton,%20WA&type=Datums*

Overland, J.E., and Walter, B.A., Jr., 1983, Marine weather of the inland waters of western Washington: Pacific Marine Environmental Laboratory, National Oceanic and Atmospheric Administration, Technical Report NOAA Technical Memorandum ERL PMEL-44.

Priesendorfer, R.W., 1988, Principal component analysis in meteorology and oceanography: Developments in Atmospheric Science, v. 17, Elsevier, Amsterdam, 425 p.

Wu, J., 1980, Wind-stress coefficients over the sea surface near neutral conditions: Journal of Physical Oceanography, v. 10, p. 727–740.

Appendix A

Table A1. Diurnal and semidiurnal tidal currents in winter and summer at the East site in Sinclair Inlet, Washington. The inclination angle (Inc) is counterclockwise from the along-inlet direction (65 degrees).

Winter Season

Depth	O1			K1		
	Amplitude	Phase	Inclination	Amplitude	Phase	Inclination
m	cm/s	degrees	degrees	cm/s	degrees	degrees
3.9	1.4	352	23	1.7	29	14
4.9	1.3	12	21	2.0	52	25
5.9	1.4	17	13	2.1	54	18
6.9	1.5	20	9	2.1	57	11
7.9	1.6	18	2	2.2	60	4
8.9	1.8	16	-4	2.3	63	-2
9.9	2.0	16	-5	2.5	64	-7
10.9	2.1	15	-4	2.6	66	-10
11.9	2.2	17	0	2.6	69	-12
12.9	2.3	19	4	2.6	72	-12
13.9	2.4	20	7	2.5	74	-13
14.9	2.4	20	5	2.4	74	-13
15.9	2.2	19	3	2.2	74	-16

Depth	M2			S2		
	Amplitude	Phase	Inclination	Amplitude	Phase	Inclination
m	cm/s	degrees	degrees	cm/s	degrees	degrees
3.9	4.2	266	-43	1.3	139	-21
4.9	4.6	273	-41	1.6	306	-41
5.9	4.8	278	-40	1.7	306	-42
6.9	4.7	285	-38	1.6	310	-43
7.9	4.5	294	-35	1.5	315	-42
8.9	4.4	303	-30	1.3	331	-31
9.9	4.1	312	-26	1.2	162	-20
10.9	4.0	139	-22	1.2	166	-12
11.9	3.8	143	-19	1.2	163	-12
12.9	3.7	146	-17	1.2	161	-14
13.9	3.5	148	-17	1.2	160	-15
14.9	3.2	151	-16	1.2	156	-18
15.9	2.8	155	-13	1.1	154	-15

Summer season

Depth	O1			K1		
	Amplitude	Phase	Inc	Amplitude	Phase	Inc
m	cm/s	degrees	degrees	cm/s	degrees	degrees
4.9	2.2	341	-3	2.7	44	24
5.9	2.6	336	-12	2.6	44	16
6.9	2.8	342	-16	2.6	43	8
7.9	2.9	347	-17	2.7	41	-1
8.9	2.9	352	-16	2.9	44	-9
9.9	2.8	354	-15	2.9	44	-15
10.9	2.8	356	-13	2.8	47	-16
11.9	2.6	358	-9	2.6	51	-13
12.9	2.6	358	-6	2.5	55	-8
13.9	2.6	357	-4	2.3	55	-3
14.9	2.4	357	-5	2.2	54	0
15.9	2.2	359	-9	2.1	53	0

Depth	M2			S2		
	Amplitude	Phase	Inc	Amplitude	Phase	Inc
m	cm/s	degrees	degrees	cm/s	degrees	degrees
4.9	5.8	245	-37	1.9	145	-9
5.9	6.0	247	-41	1.7	149	-14
6.9	5.8	253	-40	1.5	154	-20
7.9	5.4	264	-35	1.4	335	-27
8.9	5.0	279	-26	1.3	331	-33
9.9	4.8	112	-20	1.3	329	-37
10.9	4.7	120	-18	1.2	329	-38
11.9	4.5	124	-19	1.1	329	-37
12.9	4.4	126	-19	1.0	329	-30
13.9	4.3	128	-18	0.8	145	-22
14.9	4.0	132	-17	0.6	149	-16
15.9	3.6	137	-14	0.5	162	10

The average error in:
Amplitude   +_ 0.4 cm/s
Phase   +- 15 degrees
Inclination   +_ 10 degrees

Table A2. Diurnal and semidiurnal tidal currents in winter and summer at the Center site in Sinclair Inlet, Washington. The inclination angle (Inc) is counterclockwise from the along-inlet direction (65 degrees).

Winter Season

Depth	O1			K1		
	Amplitude	Phase	Inclination	Amplitude	Phase	Inclination
m	cm/s	degrees	degrees	cm/s	degrees	degrees
2.9	1.5	353	-4	2.0	5	-9
3.9	1.3	353	-4	2.0	19	-10
4.9	1.4	347	0	2.0	23	-9
5.9	1.4	341	-3	2.0	26	-8

Depth	O1			K1		
	Amplitude	Phase	Inclination	Amplitude	Phase	Inclination
m	cm/s	degrees	degrees	cm/s	degrees	degrees
6.9	1.4	335	1	1.9	28	-7
7.9	1.4	333	3	1.8	27	-5
8.9	1.2	326	10	1.7	30	-1
9.9	1.0	322	19	1.5	30	5
10.9	0.9	319	24	1.2	35	13
11.9	0.6	318	22	0.9	37	21

Depth	M2			S2		
	Amplitude	Phase	Inclination	Amplitude	Phase	Inclination
m	cm/s	degrees	degrees	cm/s	degrees	degrees
2.9	4.3	118	-6	1.3	134	-11
3.9	4.8	120	-7	1.5	135	-7
4.9	5.0	120	-5	1.6	140	-2
5.9	5.1	121	-2	1.7	145	-4
6.9	5.0	121	-1	1.6	148	-6
7.9	5.0	119	2	1.6	147	-5
8.9	4.9	117	5	1.5	145	-4
9.9	4.7	114	7	1.3	146	2
10.9	4.1	108	7	1.2	149	7
11.9	3.5	105	6	1.1	148	12

Summer season

Depth	O1			K1		
	Amplitude	Phase	Inclination	Amplitude	Phase	Inclination
m	cm/s	degrees	degrees	cm/s	degrees	degrees
3.5	1.7	352	4	3.2	39	4
4.5	1.5	347	-7	2.8	34	11
5.5	1.4	345	-2	2.5	29	12
6.5	1.7	343	1	2.0	23	11
7.5	1.6	345	3	1.5	19	10
8.5	1.4	357	6	1.0	14	11
9.5	1.1	13	15	0.5	12	35
10.5	0.8	27	29	0.4	3	87
11.5	0.7	0	70	0.7	34	-28

Depth	M2			S2		
	Amplitude	Phase	Inclination	Amplitude	Phase	Inclination
m	cm/s	degrees	degrees	cm/s	degrees	degrees
3.5	4.4	120	3	1.5	150	-13
4.5	4.9	117	5	1.4	149	-4
5.5	5.2	117	6	1.6	146	4
6.5	5.1	117	6	1.9	145	5
7.5	4.9	116	6	1.8	145	7
8.5	4.8	114	7	1.5	151	5
9.5	4.7	112	9	1.2	156	4
10.5	4.3	111	10	1.1	154	2
11.5	3.8	109	11	0.9	151	12

Table A3. Diurnal and semidiurnal tidal currents in winter and summer at the West site in Sinclair Inlet, Washington. The inclination angle (Inc) is counterclockwise from the along-inlet direction (65 degrees) The average error in the amplitude is 0.4 centimeters per second (cm/s). The average error in phase and inclination is 15 and 10 degrees.

Winter Season

Depth	O1			K1		
	Amplitude	Phase	Inclination	Amplitude	Phase	Inclination
m	cm/s	degrees	degrees	cm/s	degrees	degrees
2.9	1.6	1	-18	1.2	225	-28
3.9	1.4	5	-20	1.6	62	-22
4.9	1.1	15	-21	2.0	246	-26
5.9	0.9	14	-16	1.8	248	-32
6.9	0.8	3	-17	1.4	248	-37
7.9	0.7	350	-16	1.1	245	-43
8.9	0.5	338	-9	0.9	248	-41
9.9	0.4	312	-8	0.6	248	-45
10.9	0.3	244	6	0.3	284	-82

Depth	M2			S2		
	Amplitude	Phase	Inclination	Amplitude	Phase	Inclination
m	cm/s	degrees	degrees	cm/s	degrees	degrees
2.9	2.4	291	-26	1.5	343	-26
3.9	2.8	115	-23	1.3	338	-29
4.9	3.2	114	-17	1.0	140	-21
5.9	3.5	111	-13	0.9	124	-9
6.9	3.7	111	-11	0.9	120	-8
7.9	4.0	112	-9	0.9	123	-9
8.9	4.0	110	-8	1.0	125	-10
9.9	3.8	107	-5	0.9	130	-11
10.9	3.6	103	-1	0.9	137	-11